N O T   O N L Y

```
 333333333      000
33   3333     00   00
   33        00     00
     333     00     00
33    333     00   00
 33333333       000
```

P R O G R A M S

F O R   T H E

S I N C L A I R   Z X - 8 1

MELBOURNE HOUSE PUBLISHERS

Published by
Melbourne House (Publishers) Ltd
Glebe Cottage, Station Road
Cheddington, Leighton Buzzard
Bedfordshire LU7 7NA

ISBN 0 86161 102 0

Printed in Hong Kong.

PUBLISHER'S NOTE

We at Melbourne House are very excited to be involved with the publication of this book, making available as it does not only 30 interesting and varied programs for the SINCLAIR ZX 81 - undoubtedly the most affordable and most popular small computer in the world - but also giving the user an insight into the way the Sinclair ZX 81 can be used and filled with programming tips.

We are also publishers of other titles for the Sinclair computer, as a glance at the back pages of this book will show, ranging from titles for the complete beginner to titles of interest to more experienced users.

We have a commitment to providing literature and software for the Sinclair ZX 81, and as you will note by leafing through this book, many of the programs we publish are the result of programs that were submitted to us by ZX 81 owners.

So if you have a program or article you think would be of interest to other ZX 81 users, please write to us. We will give you a prompt assessment and reply whether the material is something we could use.

In the meantime, happy computing.

ALFRED MILGROM
PUBLISHER

INDEX

INTRODUCING THE ZX 81 : 1K

Patterns 8
Leapfrogs 10
Noughts and Crosses 14
Pinch 19
Battleships 24

GAMBLING GAMES :

Craps 28
Fruit Machine 30
Roulette 32
Horse Races 35
Blackjack 37

ZX 81 SHOWS THE WAY :

Day of the Week 44
Simple Simon 46
Kings and Queens 50
Hangman 53
Quadratic Equations 56
Simultaneous Equations 58

ARCADE GAMES :

Star Wars 62
Lunar Lander 64
Asteroids in Space 68
Bombs Away 70
U.F.O. 73
Breakout 75
Space Taxi 78

ZX 81 UTILITY PROGRAMS :

Bubble Sort 82
Line Renumbering 85
Machine Code Editor 89

CHALLENGING THE ZX 81 : 1K

Mastermind 98
Doctor ZX 81 100
Caves and Pitfalls 107
Draughts 112

INTRODUCING THE ZX 81 : 1K

* PATTERNS
* LEAPFROGS
* NOUGHTS AND CROSSES
* PINCH
* BATTLESHIPS

RANDOM PATTERNS

(c) by Neil Streeter

This program will generate thousands of interesting random patterns, stopping only when you type (BREAK).

PROGRAM STRUCTURE

The program works by randomly selecting graphics characters, and putting them in the array A$. The codes for these characters are 128 to 138. This program as well as being very pretty and quite relaxing to watch is also a good demonstration of the possible uses of the RANDOM function.

There are more graphics characters with codes 1 to 10, so by changing line 120, you can vary the patterns formed.

```
120 LET A$(X)= CHR$( INT( RND*9 +1))
```

The characters are printed repeatedly to form the patterns.

To give you time to see the pattern a PAUSE statement has been included after printing the pattern. The effect of this is to stop any computations and hold the display for the number of frames specified. Line 190 is only needed if you are running the program in fast mode.

RANDOM PATTERNS:

```
100 DIM A$(7)
110 FOR X=1 TO 7
```

```
120 LET A$(X)=CHR$( INT( RND*10 + 128))
130 NEXT X
140 FOR X=1 TO 77
150 PRINT A$;
160 NEXT X
170 PRINT A$( TO 5)
180 PAUSE 260
190 POKE 16437,255
200 CLS
210 GOTO 100
```

LEAPFROGS

The game of leapfrogs is a nice simple one:

You start off with two opposing sets of frogs, and each frog can only move to an adjacent space or leap over one frog.

```
X X X X - O O O O
1 2 3 4 5 6 7 8 9
```

So, as a first move, for example, the frog at position 4 can move to 5, or the frog at 6 can move to 5, or the frog at 3 can leap over frog 4 to land at 5, or the frog at 7 can leap over the frog at 6 to land at 5.

The object of the game is to try to get all the frogs on the left to the right, and vice versa in the least possible amount of moves. It's great fun!

STRUCTURE OF THE PROGRAM:

The first part of any program is to initialise whatever variables may be needed. In this case, we want to define the initial position of the frogs and set the number of moves taken so far to zero.

An overview of the program reveals the following structure:

```
         INITIALISE VARIABLES
PRINT    PRINT POSITION OF FROGS
         CHECK IF FINISHED
               IF YES, THEN GO TO FINISH
```

```
INPUT    ENTER PLAYER'S MOVE
         CHECK IF MOVE IS ALLOWED
               IF NOT, GO TO INPUT AGAIN
         ADD ONE TO NUMBER OF MOVES
         MAKE THE MOVE AND GO TO PRINT
FINISH   CONGRATULATE PLAYER
         ASK IF PLAYER WANT TO PLAY AGAIN
               IF YES, THEN RUN AGAIN
```

This simple "top-down" approach gives us an overview of the program and lets us understnad the program should we wish to make any changes at a later stage.

STRUCTURE OF THE VARIABLES:

For this program we shall be using "string variables" to define the position of the frogs. A string variable is easy to manipulate in this context and makes printing very fast.

We define "O$" as the original position of the frogs, and "P$" as the present position of the frogs. We can use the same variables to check if we are finished and this is done in line 150.

We use the variables "T" and "F" to represent the position "to" and "from" that the frog is moving. Because a frog can only move into an empty position we can check this easily, as in line 200.

The rest of the program is very straightforward with "C" the count of moves taken.

LEAPFROGS PROGRAM
=================

```
100  LET O$ = "■△■△■△■△△△▣△▣△▣△▣"
                These characters are obtained
```

```
                by using upper case "SPACE" and
                "P" while in GRAPHICS mode.
110  LET P$ = O$
120  LET C = 0
130  CLS
140  PRINT P$,,,"1△2△3△4△5△6△7△8△
   9",,,"ENTER MOVE"
150  IF P$(1 TO 7) = O$(11 TO 17) AND P$(11 TO
17) = O$(1 TO 7) THEN GO TO 250
160  INPUT A$
170  IF A$ = "" THEN STOP
180  LET F = 2*( CODE A$ (1) - 28) - 1
190  LET T = 2*( CODE A$ (2) - 28) - 1
200  IF P$(T) <> "△"  OR ABS (T - F) > 4 THEN
   GOTO 160
210  LET C = C + 1
220  LET P$(T) = P$(F)
230  LET P$(F) = "△"
240  GOTO 130
250  PRINT "YOU DID IT IN△";C;"△MOVES"
   ,,,"ANOTHER GO?"
260  INPUT A$
270  IF CODE A$ = 62 THEN RUN
```

NOTE:

The symbol "△" is used to indicate the need for a space at that position. This symbol is not used everywhere a space is required, but only in those positions where the numbers of spaces is critical to the running of the program or to legibility of the display, as in lines 100 and 250 in the above program.

RUNNING THE PROGRAM:

The program expects a 2-digit input to define to move "from" and the move "to".

It will therefore only accept as a valid first

entry one of the the following moves:

35 45 65 75

Happy leapfrogging!

NOUGHTS AND CROSSES

We have all played Noughts and Crosses in our time, and this time the challenge is to beat the computer.

The computer in this program is a little greedy in that it refuses to let you start, but then again, it's not like your next-door neighbour. It is always available for a game!

The screen display is as follows:

1	2	3
8	X	4
7	6	5

You enter your move by choosing the number where you wish to move to.

The programmer is so confident of his program that you will notice there is only provision for the computer to win or to concede a draw!

NOUGHTS AND CROSSES:

```
 50  PAUSE S * Z
 60  CLS
 70  LET A$ = "1 ▌△ 2 ▌△ 38 ▌△ X ▌△ 47 ▌△
        6 ▌△ 5"            (graphics 8 followed
                            by space)
 80  FOR I = X TO X + Y
 90  PRINT A$ ( TO B-X )
100  IF I =< Y THEN PRINT "▄▄█▄▄█▄▄"
                           (graphics 6,Q,6,6,Q,66)
```

```
110  LET A$ = A$ ( B TO )
120  NEXT I
130  FOR T = X TO Z
140  PRINT AT B,X ; "YOUR TURN"
150  LET V = 52
160  INPUT R
170  GOSUB 420
180  PRINT AT B,X ; "MY TURN △ △ "
190  IF T > X THEN GOTO 230
200  LET E = R = Y * INT (R/Y)
210  LET P = R
220  LET A = P - P
230  LET V = 61
240  LET A = A + X
250  IF T = X OR P = R + Z OR P = R - Z
       THEN GOTO 300
260  LET P = P + Z
270  GOSUB S * Z
280  PRINT "I WON"
290  GOTO X
300  IF A = X + Y AND E THEN LET A = B - X
310  IF A = Z THEN LET A = Z + Y
320  LET P = P + A
330  GOSUB S * Z
340  IF A = B - X THEN GOTO 280
350  NEXT T
360  PRINT "DRAW"
370  GOTO X
400  IF P > B THEN LET P = P - B
410  LET R = P
420  LET D = PEEK 16396 + 256 * PEEK 16397
430  FOR I = X TO Z*B + B
440  IF PEEK (D+I) = R + 28 THEN POKE D+I, V
450  NEXT I
460  RETURN
```

It should be obvious to you looking at line 50 that the program would crash if you were to press (RUN) (NEW LINE). This is because we have some undefined variables, such as S and Z.

The reason these variables are used in the program is to save space, and the variables need to be defined before we can play Naughts and Crosses. One way to do this is used in many other programs in this book - use 2 programs, the first program to define the variables, (RUN) it, and then enter the second program with the variables stored in memory.

We could use this same method in this program, but instead we will use the second method of defining the variables after the main program has been entered.

We can do this by entering BASIC lines without line numbers, and pressing (NEW LINE). This tells the operating system we wish to execute that instruction immediately.

In this program, after you have entered the listing above, enter the following lines without line numbers, and press (NEW LINE) after each line has been entered:

```
LET X = 1
LET Y = 2
LET Z = 4
LET B = 8
LET S = 100
```

All the variables have been defined. We still cannot press (RUN) as this will clear the variables from memory. Enter (GOTO 1) (NEW LINE).

Structure of the Program:

You may find it difficult to follow the structure of this program because its logic is fairly well hidden and the use of variables in the listing makes it difficult to know what is happening.

Lines 70 to 120 draw the Naughts and Crosses board. Note that this is the only time in the program that the board is drawn up. All changes to the board which occur later involve changing only the piece that is to be moved.

The variable T in line 130 indicates TURN and after each player has had 4 turns, the game must be a draw (see line 360). This is obvious as after 4 turns 8 spaces will be filled up and the computer's first turn has already been made = all 9 possible positions have been filled.

When it is the player's turn, we obtain R (REPLY) and go to subroutine 420. This subroutine looks at the first 40 squares of the screen display and replaces the number entered by the letter 'O'. This effectively finishes the player's turn.

If it is the computer's first turn (T = 1) there is some preliminaries we have to do: remember the PREVIOUS move (variable P), set the ADD factor (variable A) to zero, and determine if the player started on an EVEN (variable E) number or odd.

Note that the board is defined in such a way that all corner moves are represented by an odd number and all side moves are even numbers! The other feature of interest is that a blocking move is either +4 or -4 the original move. In other words if the computer moves to square 1, you will need to move to square 5 to stop it making 3 in a row.

If it is the computer's first move or if the player has blocked successfully (line 250) then the computer cannot yet claim victory (GOTO 300). On the other hand, if it is a win the computer fills in the appropriate square, claims victory and jumps back to the beginning.

The computer's sequence of moves is determined by PREVIOUS and ADD. The computer's first move will always be to the right clockwise of the player's first move (PREVIOUS + 1). Its next move will be 2 to the right clockwise from that (PREVIOUS + 2), and so on. Lines 300 and 310 take care of the exception where ADD is not automatically incremented by 1.

That's it. Good luck.

PINCH

This is a one dimensional version of the Japanese game Go. This is one of the few games in this book where it is not possible for a player to play alone or against the computer.

Nonetheless we have included it in this book because it is such an interesting and challenging game. At the end of this listing we also make suggestions on how to teach the computer to play PINCH, but you will need additional memory for that.

The rules of the game of PINCH first appeared in Scientific American in 1980. (As mentioned above it is a 2-dimensional version of GO, and was included in a discussion of possible 2 dimensional games, including 2 dimensional Chess!)

Two players take turns to place stones on a 9 position board. You can capture a connected group of your opponent's stones by surrounding them on both sides. The board appears like this:

```
- - X O - - - - O
1 2 3 4 5 6 7 8 9
```

If it is X to move, placing a stone at 5 would capture the stone at 4. Placing a stone at 8 would capture the stone at 9. On the other hand placing a stone at 6 would have no effect.

It is illegal to make a suicidal move, but you can go into what would normally be a suicidal position if that results in the capture of opposing stones.

There is only one other rule, and that is that it is illegal to make a move which would make the positions exactly the same as they had been after your last turn. This is a rule which this program does not check for.

PROGRAM STRUCTURE

The structure of the main program is:

```
     Initialize varaibles
MOVE Print the board
     Print the player's move
     If possible, kill opponents groups
     If possible, kill player's groups
     If the move was legal, goto MOVE
     Give the player another turn
```

B is the current player. The subroutine at 500 checks which groups not belonging to B are dead and removes them. The ends are regarded as belonging to B.

After the subroutine has been run once, B is changed, and the subroutine checks for a suicidal move.

```
        Initialize variables
        Go to NEXT B
FIND    Find a stone of B's
        Set equal to S
NEXT B  Increment P until a blank or
           another of B's stones is found.
        If a blank go to FIND
        Kill stones between S and P
```

PINCH:

```
100 LET A$="-▲-▲-▲-▲-▲-▲-▲-▲-▲-" (10 -'s)
```

```
110 LET B$="OX"
120 LET B=1
130 CLS
140 PRINT A$( TO 17)
150 PRINT "1 2 3 4 5 6 7 8 9"
160 PRINT AT 5,B-B;"PLAYER ";B;"?"
170 INPUT S
180 LET A$(2*S-B/B)=B$(B)
190 PRINT AT B-B,B-B;A$( TO 17)
200 LET D=B-B
210 GOSUB 500
220 LET B=INT ((B+1)/B)
230 LET D=-D
240 GOSUB 500
250 IF D<=B-B THEN GOTO 130
260 GOTO 220
500 LET A$(19)=B$(B)
510 LET P=-1
520 GOTO 560
530 LET P=P+2
540 IF P>=19 THEN RETURN
550 IF A$(P)<>B$(B) OR A$(P+2)=B$(B)
      THEN GOTO 530
560 LET S=P
570 LET P=P+2
580 IF A$(P)="-" THEN GOTO 530
590 IF A$(P)<>B$(B) AND P<19 THEN GOTO 570
600 IF P>B/B THEN LET D=D+B/B
610 FOR K=S+2 TO P-2 STEP 2
620 LET A$(K)="-"
630 NEXT K
640 GOTO 540
```

NOTES:

You may realise from looking at this program that it only just fits into the 1K machine. There are therefore attempts to minimise any waste of memory.

One simple way to do this is to eliminate all

references to the number 1 or 0 in the listing as these both take up 6 bytes. Instead we use B/B for 1, and B-B for 0 - both of these only require 3 bytes.

Line 220 gives a simple way of switching between 1 and 2. If B was 1, the result will be B=2, while if B was 2 the result will be B=1!

RUNNING THE PROGRAM

As it is illegal to move to a position where you will immediately be captured unless you can capture some of your opponents stones by the move. If you do make an illegal move, the group of stones will be removed, and it will still be your move.

The computer does not play this game, but provides for two players to compete, removing dead stones for them. This is an interesting, and constantly changing game. The stategies involved should keep you thinking for a while.

IMPROVING THE PROGRAM:

The basic strategy of the game is to ensure that you can capture whenever possible and not walk into a trap!

The subroutine at line 500 at present kills any group located betwen enemies.

It is quite easy to adapt this subroutine to merely check if a group would be killed and if so how many men removed.

The strategy for a computer to play would therefore be something along the lines:

```
For all possible squares
      Check how many enemies would be
        killed by this move
      Check how many of one's own men
        would be killed by this move.
Next move.
```

As there are only 9 possible squares to go to, this should not take too long to compute. Then choose the move which would kill most enemies. If no such move exists, choose a move which would not result in suicide.

Once this is working, a further improvement would be to check whether the move just made would make it easy for the enemy to capture on the next move (a simple version of look ahead).

You are going to need all your computer concentration for this one.

BATTLESHIPS

World War II has been declared. As you sit at the console of your submarine, the captain alerts you that Intelligence reports 4 battleships in the general area.

Radar is out! You must bomb the seas and hope to find the battleships before they find you!

Each ship occupies two adjacent spaces on your 9 x 9 grid: Enter the coordinates and the boys in the missile room will send a torpedo hurtling to that point.

If you've hit a ship, an 'X' will appear on the console - otherwise only 'O'. When you've hit all ships in the area, the captain orders a move to a new part of the Atlantic.

PROGRAM STRUCTURE:

```
           Randomly choose the positions
                   of the 4 battleships
           Print the grid
   BOMB    Get the position to be bombed
           If a ship is there,
              then print an 'X' there
                   and if there have been 8 hits
                       then run the program again
           Otherwise, print a 'O'.
           Go to BOMB again.
```

The array X contains the position of the 4 battleships (2 positions on the grid for each ship). The player's input is checked against each of these. Grid position 4,1 is stored as 41 and

printed at 8,2 on the screen (the extra spaces between lines aids readability).

The number of hits is stored in H, and when 8 hits have been recorded the game is started afresh.

BATTLESHIPS:

```
100  LET H = 0
110  DIM X(8)
120  FOR R = 1 TO 8 STEP 2
130  LET X(R) = INT (RND*8 + 1)*10 +
       INT (RND*9 + 1)
140 LET X(R+1) = X(R) + 10
150  NEXT R
160  CLS
170  PRINT " △△1△2△3△4△5△6△
       7△8△9"
       (2 spaces at the beginning, then a
        single space between each number)
180  FOR R = 1 TO 9
190  PRINT AT 2*R, R-R; R
200  NEXT R
210  INPUT M
220  FOR R = 1 TO 8
230  IF M = X (R) THEN GOTO 300
240  NEXT R
250  PRINT AT INT (M/10) * 2, (M - INT(M/10)
       *10) * 2; "O"
260  GOTO 210
300  PRINT AT INT (M/10) * 2, (M - INT(M/10)
       *10) * 2; "X"
310  LET H = H + 1
320  IF H = 8 THEN RUN
330  GOTO 210
```

RUNNING THE PROGRAM:

When you press (RUN) (NEW LINE), the screen will be blank and two axes will show the numbers 1 to 9. This is your bombing grid.

The ZX81 will be waiting for a number input from you to bomb. A 2 digit number is required, with the vertical axis the first number -
  e.g. enter 52 if you want to bomb the position 5 rows down and 2 columns across.

You should be able to locate all the ships in about 40 turns. When all have been bombed, a new set of axes will be drawn, with the ships now hidden at different locations.

GAMBLING GAMES

* CRAPS
* FRUIT MACHINE
* ROULETTE
* HORSE RACES
* BLACKJACK

CRAPS

(c) by Neil Streeter

This program simulates the dice game 'craps'

If you throw a 7 or 11 on your first throw, you win immediately. A score of 2, 3 or 12 on your first throw means you lose.If you throw anything else you get another throw.

On subsequent throws, you win by matching your first throw, or lose by throwing a 7.

This is an easy and fun game to play: just type 'Y' to continue playing and the computer does the rest. It even throws the dice for you.

PROGRAM STRUCTURE

The throwing of the dice is simulated by using the RND function. Throwing a single die can be simulated by

```
LET C= INT (RND * 6)+1
```

and throwing two dice by

```
LET C= INT (RND *6)+ INT (RND * 6)+2
```

Note that this is not the same as

```
LET C= INT (RND * 11)+2
```

although both give a random number between 2 and 12.

CRAPS:

```
100 CLS
110 PRINT"CRAPS"
```

```
130 LET J=0
140 LET C= INT (RND*6)+ INT (RND*6) +2
150 LET J=J+1
160 IF J=1 THEN GOTO 210
170 IF C=D THEN GOTO 340
180 IF C=7 THEN GOTO 360
190 PRINT"YOU SCOREΔ";C
200 GOTO 140
210 IF C=7 OR C=11 THEN GOTO 250
220 IF C=2 OR C=3 OR C=12 THEN GOTO 270
230 LET D=C
240 GOTO 190
250 PRINT"SCOREΔ";C;"ΔAND WIN"
260 GOTO 280
270 PRINT"SCOREΔ";C;"ΔAND LOSE"
280 PRINT
290 PRINT"TYPE ""Y"" TO CONTINUE"
300 INPUT L$
310 IF L$<>"Y" THEN STOP
320 PRINT
330 GOTO 100
340 PRINT"SCOREΔ"; C ;
      "ΔAND WIN BY MATCHING"
350 GOTO 280
360 PRINT"SCOREΔ";C;"ΔAND LOSE"
370 GOTO 280
```

Happy gambling!

FRUIT MACHINE

(c) by Neil Streeter

This program simulates a fruit machine, just like those in Los Vegas.

You start with $10, and it costs 50c to play a game. The names of three objects will appear on the screen. If they are all the same, you win, and the computer will credit you with your winnings. Otherwise it will subtract the cost of the game. You can play again by entering (NEW LINE), until you run out of money: unlike your favourite casino the computer does not give credit.

STRUCTURE OF THE PROGRAM:

The randomizing function (RND) is used to generate either a bar, an orange or a cherry. Line 20 generates a number 1 <= N < 10.

If N < 2, a bar is generated, if 2 < N < 5, an orange, otherwise, a cherry, This gives a weghting heavily favouring the cherries. If you don't like the odds, that's the line to change.

INITIALIZE VARIABLES
GENERATE OBJECTS RANDOMLY
CHECK IF PLAYER HAS WON
     IF HE HASN'T CHECK IF HE HAS ANY MONEY LEFT
OTHERWISE CREDIT WINNINGS

VARIABLES:

The money you have is stored in M

B,A,and C contain the number of bars, oranges, and cherries in the current game.

FRUIT MACHINE:

```
30  LET M=10
40  LET B=0
50  LET A=0
60  LET C=0
70  FOR I=1 TO 3
80  LET N=(RND*9+1)
90  IF N>2 THEN GOTO 130
100 PRINT "BAR▵";
110 LET A=A+1
120 GOTO 190
130 IF N>5 THEN GOTO 170
140 PRINT "ORANGE▵";
150 LET B=B+1
160 GOTO 190
170 PRINT "CHERRY▵";
180 LET C=C+1
190 NEXT I
200 IF A=3 OR B=3 OR C=3 THEN GOTO 250
210 PRINT AT 4,4;"TOO BAD...YOU LOSE"
220 LET M=M-.5
230 IF M<=.1 THEN GOTO 340
240 GOTO 280
250 PRINT AT 4,10;"YOU WIN"
260 LET M=M+A*2/3+B/2+C/3
280 PRINT
290 PRINT "YOU NOW HAVE $";M
310 PRINT "TO PLAY AGAIN PRESS NEWLINE."
315 INPUT A$
320 CLS
330 GOTO 40
340 PRINT "YOU HAVE LOST ALL YOUR MONEY"
```

ROULETTE

(c) by Alistair Ogilvy

A gambler's delight: - You start with $100 to bet on the roulette wheel. You can place your money on a range of values (between 1 and 36) or odds or evens.

Then the wheel begins to spin. The numbers flash onto the screen until the wheel stops. The computer then calculates how much you have won or lost, and adjusts the total of your money.

You'd better be careful with this one - you could lose everything!

PROGRAM STRUCTURE

The numbers are generated by RND. To simulate the spinning of the wheel, 15 numbers are generated and successively printed at the same position.

In line 370, the expression

IF (K AND C)

is used. This is true if K and C are both non-zero.

ROULETTE:

```
100 LET M=100
105 PAUSE 100
108 CLS
110 LET C=2
115 PRINT "HIGH?"
120 INPUT H
130 PRINT H,,"LOW?";
```

```
140 INPUT L
150 PRINT L
160 IF H<=L OR L<1 THEN GOTO 105
170 IF H<=36 THEN GOTO 206
190 PRINT "O=ODDS OR 1=EVENS"
200 INPUT C
205 LET H=17+L
206 LET O=INT (36/(H-L))
208 PRINT "ODDS=1 INΔ";O
210 PRINT "$";M,"ΔBET$"
220 INPUT B
230 PRINT B
250 FOR I=1 TO 15
260 LET A=INT (37*RND)
265 PRINT AT 9,0;A;"Δ"
267 NEXT I
270 IF C<>2 THEN GOTO 360
280 IF A<=H AND A>=L THEN GOTO 330
290 PRINT "LOST"
300 LET M=M-B
310 IF M<=0 THEN GOTO 500
320 GOTO 105
330 LET P=O*B - B
340 PRINT "WON $";P
345 LET M=M+P
350 GOTO 105
360 LET K=INT (A/2=INT (A/2))
370 IF (K AND C) OR (K=C AND C=0)
      THEN GOTO 330
390 GOTO 290
500 PRINT "LOST ALL"
```

RUNNING THE PROGRAM:

When the program commences, you are going to be asked for the number range you wish to bet on: Choose any high limit and any low limit.

For example, you could bet on all numbers from 1 to 12 or only from 30 to 34.

If you wish instead to bet on odds or evens, simply enter a number greater than 36 in answer to the query for the high number, and any number smaller than that for low. The computer will then ask whether you want odds or evens.

The odds will be calculated (to a round number) and displayed so that you can place your bet.

The croupier will obligingly wait until you have placed your bet before spinning the wheel.

HORSE RACES

(c) by Neil Streeter

This program simulates a three horse race. You have $500 to begin with and you can bet on any horse. All horses have an equal chance of winning. The game ends when you have lost all your money.

PROGRAM STRUCTURE

The path of each horse is shown by a black bar. The horse with the longest bar is winning. This is done by using the PLOT function to fill in his present position. The race ends as soon as one horse reaches position 31.

The RND function generates a number between 0 and 1. This is multiplied by 3 and added to 1. The integer part of this is then 1,2 or 3. The horse thus chosen is allowed to advance one space.

Note the use of RAND.The function RND always uses the same sequence of numbers. That is, it doesn't really generate random numbers, but returns a pseudo-random number, a number which appears to be random. For many purposes this is sufficient, but in this program, that would mean that it would become predictable which horse would win.

RAND causes RND to start at different places in its sequence of numbers each time. This is closer to a RANDOM random number generator.

HORSE RACE:

```
105 LET E=500
110 PRINT "BET?"
115 INPUT B
120 PRINT B
122 PRINT "HORSE (1-3)?"
125 INPUT H
130 CLS
135 PRINT "1","ΔΔ"
136 PRINT "2","ΔΔFINISH"
138 PRINT "3","ΔΔ"
140 LET W=2
145 LET X=2
150 LET Y=2
160 RAND
200 LET R=INT (RND*3+1)
210 IF R=1 THEN LET W=W+1
220 IF R=2 THEN LET X=X+1
230 IF R=3 THEN LET Y=Y+1
250 PLOT W,43
260 PLOT X,41
270 PLOT Y,39
290 IF X=31 OR Y=31 OR W=31 THEN GOTO 350
300 GOTO 200
350 IF W=31 AND H=1 THEN GOTO 450
360 IF X=31 AND H=2 THEN GOTO 450
370 IF Y=31 AND H=3 THEN GOTO 450
390 LET E=E-B
400 PRINT AT 5,0;"MONEY=";E
410 IF E<=0 THEN STOP
420 GOTO 110
450 LET E=E+B*2
460 GOTO 400
```

BLACKJACK

(c) by Alistair Ogilvy

This is the traditional card game, and it all fits into the unexpanded 1K ZX81. It even keeps track of the card totals, how much money you have bet and how much you have left. And naturally, it won't let you bet more than you have.

The ZX81 dealer asks you how much you want to bet, then deals himself a card, and then deals you a card. You are then asked if you want a HIT? (ie. do you want another card?). Any answer such as Y or YES or even pressing NEWLINE will be yes, while N or NO or NEVER! will be taken to mean you don't want another card.

If your card total is over 21, you've lost. If you stop before you BUST then the dealer will deal himself more cards. The dealer always draws below 16 and sits on 17 and above.

The amount of money you have left will be shown and you will be invited to bet again.

Step right up, ladies and gentlemen!

STRUCTURE OF THE PROGRAM:

As you can imagine, it's not easy to fit such a complex program into the unexpanded ZX81. We have to resort to two space saving techiques:

1. Defining variables in another program first.
2. Replacing as many numbers as possible in the program listing by variables.

The second method can chop as much as 100 bytes off a program like this because each number in a program line takes up 6 bytes as opposed to one byte for a variable. Admittedly the variable takes 7 bytes in memory in the first place, but if you use the same numbers a lot there is considerable savings possible.

PROGRAM 1:
==========

This program defines the variables we need - mainly predefining 'A' as a variable and the string variable B$ which defines the cards in the pack.

The other variables are the numbers most commonly used in Program 2: X=1, Y=2, Z=10, and T=21.

```
100  LET X = 1
110  LET Y = 2
120  LET Z = 10
130  LET T = 21
140  LET B$ = "N23456789TAJQK"
150  LET A = 0
```

Note that in the definition of cards we used the letter 'T' to denote the '10' - this enables us to display all cards as a single letter.

Once this program is entered, press (RUN) and (NEW LINE). This will save the variables in memory and the listing of this program is therefore no longer required.

PROGRAM 2:
==========

This is the program that does all the work - indeed if you have additional memory you would not need Program 1. (All you would need to do is

to replace all references to X by 1, etc.,.. and include the lines defining A and B$ in the main program).

The structure of this program is as follows:

```
NEW BET INPUT PLAYER'S BET
           IF NO MONEY LEFT, STOP
        DEAL FIRST CARD TO DEALER AND PLAYER
        FOR PLAYER AND FOR DEALER:
            IF PLAYER ASK IF CARD WANTED
                IF SWITCH TO DEALER
            DEAL THE CARD AND PRINT IT
            CALCULATE VALUE OF HAND AND PRINT IT
            IF OVER 21 GO TO PAYOUT
            IF DEALER AND OVER 16 GO TO PAYOUT
PAYOUT  IF PLAYER BUST, MONEY WON = 0
        IF DEALER < 21 AND DEALER TOTAL <= PLAYER
            TOTAL THEN MONEY WON = 0
        MONEY = MONEY + MONEY WON
        GO TO NEW BET AGAIN
```

As you can see from the above structure there was insufficient room in the 1K version to allow for greater payout if the player makes Blackjack, or to allow the player to win if he gets '5 and under'. If you have additional memory you can easily write those provisions in.

The numbering in this program is slightly non-standard: this has been done deliberately to allow the use of variables in GOTO and GOSUB statements. We therefore start at line 90 and have the unusual line 125.

```
 90  LET M = Z * Z
100  DIM P (Y+Y)
110  PRINT AT Z,X; "$"; M ;" ▲ BET?"
120  INPUT B
125  CLS
130  IF B > M THEN STOP
```

```
140  LET M = M - B
150  PRINT "ΔΔYOU"; TAB Z; "ZX81"
160  FOR I = Y TO X STEP - X
170  GOSUB T * T
180  NEXT I
190  FOR I = X TO Y
200  LET A = P(I) = X + Z
210  IF I = X THEN PRINT AT Z,X; "HIT?"
220  IF I = X THEN INPUT A$
230  PRINT AT Z,X; "ΔΔΔΔ"
240  IF I = X AND CODE A$ = CODE B$ THEN GOTO 280
250  GOSUB T * T
260  IF P(I) > T OR (I=Y AND P(I) > 16) THEN
       GOTO 290
270  GOTO T * Z
280  NEXT I
290  IF (P(Y) <= T AND P(Y) >= P(X) ) OR
       P(X) > T THEN LET B = B - B
300  LET M = M + B + B
310  GOTO Z * Z
500  LET P(I+Y) = P(I+Y) + X
510  LET C = INT (13 * RND) + Y
520  IF C = Z + X THEN LET A = A + X
530  LET P(I) = P(I) + C * ( C < Z+Y ) +
       Z * ( C > Z+X )
540  IF P(I) < T+X OR A = X - X THEN GOTO 570
550  LET A = A - X
560  LET P(I) = P(I) - Z
570  PRINT AT X+Y, Y * P(I+Y) + Z * (I=Y); B$(C)
580  PRINT AT Y+Y, Z * I - Z + Y ;P(I)
590  RETURN
```

Special Notes:

You will notice a strange notation in line 200, where A = P(I) = 11. The variable A is being used in this program to keep track of the number of aces in the player's hand, and what the line says is: Let A = 1 if the value in the hand is 11.

The long way to write this is

```
IF P(I) = 11 THEN LET A = 1
```

But we know that the value of an expression such as P(I) = 11 will be 1 if true and 0 if false.

We can therefore write

```
LET A = ( P(I) = 11 )
```

And as you can see from the program listing, the brackets are not necessary.

The other line you may find odd is line 530 where the value of the player's hand is being calculated. The card just drawn (variable C) can be anywhere from 2 to 14.

If the value is 2 - 10, we want to add that value.

If the value is 11 (ace) we also want to add that value, as long as we are not bust. (That possiblity is taken care of in lines 540 - 560).

If the value is 12 - 14 (ie. we have drawn J, Q, or K) then we want to add 10.

The one line 530 does all this for us: it says add the value of the card if the value is less than 12 and add 10 if the value is over 11. Simple, isn't it!

You may also have noticed that we use GOSUB T * T (which means 21 * 21 = 441) and yet no line 441 exits. This is fine because the program will go to whichever is the first allowed line after the number specified (in this case 500).

RUNNING THE PROGRAM:

Because we need to remember the variables we saved in the first program, we cannot use (RUN) or (CLEAR) at any stage because that will destroy our carefully saved variables.

It is therefore necessary to use (GOTO 1) (NEW LINE).

The program works exceptionally well in SLOW mode, so if you are loading the program from tape (which will automatically set the mode to FAST) you will have to enter the SLOW instruction in first.

Because of space limitations, the program is a little terse. The screen will first show:

```
        $100 BET?
```

This means you have $100 to bet with and how much would you like to wager?

The screen will then show something like:

```
     YOU          ZX81
     T            8
     10           8
     HIT?
```

This means that you have drawn a '10' (value of your hand is underneath your cards = 10) and the dealer has drawn an '8' (value of hand = 8). Do you want another card.

Of course the answer is yes, and there goes another evening spent in mad compulsive gambling.

ZX 81 SHOWS THE WAY

* DAY OF THE WEEK
* SIMPLE SIMON
* KINGS AND QUEENS
* HANGMAN
* QUADRATIC EQUATIONS
* SIMULTANEOUS EQUATIONS

DAY OF THE WEEK

Enter your birth date , and the ZX 81 will tell you on which day of the week you were born.

If you think you are more than 280 years old, this program is not for you. The computer is not that silly.

PROGRAM STRUCTURE

The character strings corresponding to each day of the week are stored one after the other in D$. The day of the week is calculated as a number between 0 and 6. This is multiplied by 3, and 1 is added. This gives the position of the first letter in the name of the day. The day is printed by PRINT D$(Z TO Z+2)

DAY OF THE WEEK:

```
110 LET D$="SUNMONTUEWEDTHUFRISAT"
120 PRINT"PLEASE ENTER YOUR NAME"
130 INPUT A$
140 PRINT "HELLO ";A$
150 PRINT "ENTER DATE OF BIRTH","DAY",
160 INPUT D
170 IF D<1 OR D>31 THEN GOTO 160
180 PRINT D,"MONTH",
190 INPUT M
200 PRINT M,"YEAR"
210 INPUT Y
220 IF Y<1700 THEN GOTO 450
230 CLS
300 LET K=0
310 IF M<3 THEN LET K=1
```

```
320 LET L=Y-K
330 LET O=M+12*K
340 LET P=INT (L/100)
350 LET Z=INT (13*(O+1)/5) +
      INT ((5*L)/4) - P+INT(P/4) + D-1
360 LET Z=(Z-7*INT (Z/7))*3+1
400 PRINT A$;"ΔWAS BORN ONΔ";D$(Z TO Z+2)
410 STOP
450 PRINT A$;"ΔIS TOO OLD"
```

SIMPLE SIMON

"Simple Simon" is the computer successor to the age-old game of "Simon Says". In the computer version, a letter or number is displayed one at a time on the screen and the player has to correctly type in the sequence of letters and numbers as they appeared.

As the number of letters that has appeared on the screen increases, the letters (or numbers) flash on to the screen more and more quickly.

This program will also make use of the fact that in the Sinclair ZX81 the character generator is located in software and use this information to display each letter in large (8 lines deep) size.

On many other computers the character generator (that is whatever it is in the computer that defines what each letter of the alphabet will look like on the screen) is handled by a special chip. In the Sinclair ZX81 all that information is stored in the ROM (Read Only Memory), which also contains the operating system.

If you look at your screen closely enough, you will be able to see that each letter on the screen (and even the graphics characters) are made up of little dots closely joined up. In fact each character space on the screen has room for 64 dots (an array of 8 lines of 8 dots each), and the information about which dots are to be on and which are to be off is stored at memory location 7680 onwards.

The information about each letter of the alphabet (and each graphic character and number) can be

stored in 8 bytes of memory. This is because each byte of memory has 8 bits and the ZX81 uses each bit to indicate a different position on the screen.

We will first of all display this ability to have larger than life characters in the following short program -

DISPLAYING LARGE CHARACTERS:

```
100  LET A$ = "■"          (graphics space)
110  LET B$ = "▵"          (space)
120  FOR X = 28 TO 63
130  FOR L = 1 TO 8
140  LET V = PEEK (7679 + L + 8*X)
150  LET P$ = ""           (empty string)
160  LET D = 256
170  FOR K = 8 TO 1 STEP -1
180  LET D = D / 2
190  LET C$ = B$
200  IF V < D THEN GOTO 230
210  LET C$ = A$
220  LET V = V - D
230  LET P$ = P$ + C$
240  NEXT K
250  PRINT P$
260  NEXT L
270  PAUSE 60
280  CLS
290  NEXT X
```

Quite obviously the meat of this program is in lines 130 - 260:

The variable L is used to indicated which line of the character we are to print next, and K is the appropriate dot. It is in line 140 that we obtain the information about the line to be printed - we PEEK into memory to see which dots should be

'on'. If the dot is to be 'on, then we will be print a black square (as defined by A$).

This program demonstrates the method used in the large printing and will allow you to see how the eye can often be fooled if the print is small enough.

In the program above, the display of the large print character was done while you were watching it. This had two effects : 1. the display was quite slow to come up and 2. there was no chance of missing what the character was. In the program "Simple Simon" we will switch to FAST mode so that you won't see the character being built up on the screen, and then switch to SLOW for your input.

SIMPLE SIMON:

```
100  LET A$ = "█"              (graphics space)
110  LET B$ = "▵"              (space)
120  LET Y$ = ""               (empty string)
130  FOR G = 1 TO 20
140  LET X = 28 + INT (36*RND)
150  LET Y$ = Y$ + CHR$ X
160  FAST
170  FOR L = 1 TO 8
180  LET V = PEEK (7679 + L + 8*X)
190  LET P$ = ""               (empty string)
200  LET D = 256
210  FOR K = 8 TO 1 STEP -1
220  LET D = D / 2
230  LET C$ = B$
240  IF V < D THEN GOTO 270
250  LET C$ = A$
260  LET V = V - D
270  LET P$ = P$ + C$
280  NEXT K
290  PRINT P$
```

```
300  NEXT L
310  SLOW
320  PAUSE 70 - 3*G
330  CLS
340  INPUT Z$
350  IF Y$ <> Z$ THEN GOTO 370
360  NEXT G
370  PRINT "YOU SAID ▲"; Z$
380  PRINT Y$ ; "▲ IS RIGHT"
```

The structure of this program is very simple to follow, once you have seen the Large Print Program. Note that the amount of time the character is displayed is reduced as you go along. Remember the sequence of 20 letters and numbers correctly, and you've won!

KINGS AND QUEENS OF ENGLAND

This program uses a 'multiple choice' format to test your knowledge of history. You will be asked who was reigning in a particular year, and given three answers from which to select. You then type the number of the answer, and the computer will tell you if you are right or not.

PROGRAM STRUCTURE

```
Initialize variables
FOR J = 1 TO 3
     select a date
     find the king who reigned then
NEXT J
select one of the 3 dates
print question and choices
check the answer
run the program again
```

The kings and the years of their death are stored in the string, Z$. The entry for each king is 7 characters long - padded with blanks if necessary. When a date has been chosen, each entry is checked until one is found where the king died after the chosen year.

The next entry is obtained by adding 7 to the position of the character that was previously being considered.

B$ is a two dimensional array used to store the names of the 3 kings offered as choices. B$(1,1) refers to the first character in the first name. B$(1) refers to the whole of that name.

Note that the program is run again at the end. RUN does not clear the screen, so the question remains on the screen while the computer selects the next question. This gives you time to see the answer given by the computer.

KINGS AND QUEENS OF ENGLAND:

```
100 LET Z$="1087W1△1100W2△1135H1△1154ST△1189H2 △
      1199R1△1216J△△1272H3△1307ED11327ED21377ED
      31399R2△1413H4△1422H5△1461H6△"
110 DIM P(3)
120 DIM B$(3,3)
130 RAND
140 FOR J=1 TO 3
150 LET P(J)=INT (RND*396 + 1065)
160 LET X$="0000"
170 LET I=J/J
180 LET X$=Z$(I TO I+3)
190 LET I=I+7
200 IF VAL(X$)<=P(J) THEN GOTO 180
210 LET B$(J)=Z$(I-3 TO I-1)
220 NEXT J
230 LET N=INT (RND*3 + J/J)
240 CLS
250 PRINT "WHO REIGNED IN△";P(N),"1△";B$(J/J);"
    △△2△";B$(2);"△△3△";B$(3)
260 INPUT X
270 IF B$(X)=B$(N) THEN PRINT "YES"
280 IF B$(X)<>B$(N) THEN PRINT "NO△";B$(N)
290 RUN
```

Take especial care in entering Line 100! Rememeber the format we are using : for each monarch, we enter the date of his death, then a three letter code for the monarch's name. Each entry therefore has 7 characters (where the abbreviation is less than 3 characters, we make it up to three by adding spaces).

RUNNING THE PROGRAM

This program will keep on running forever unless you type break or input an illegal value. You will be asked who reigned in a particular year, and three possible answers will be given.

It is possible that not all of these answers will not be different. You will still be marked correctly, no matter which of the correct answers you choose. If the king died in the given year (so that there were 2 kings in that year) choose the new king.

If you select the wrong answer, the correct answer will be printed on the screen.

KINGS AND QUEENS OF ENGLAND Part 1:

W1	1066 - 1087	Norman
W2	1087 - 1100	
H1	1100 - 1135	
St	1135 - 1154	
H2	1154 - 1189	Plantaganet
R1	1189 - 1199	
J	1199 - 1216	
H3	1216 - 1272	
Ed1	1272 - 1307	
Ed2	1307 - 1327	
Ed3	1327 - 1377	
R2	1377 - 1399	
H4	1399 - 1413	Lancaster
H5	1413 - 1422	
H6	1422 - 1461	

HANGMAN

This is a game for two players. One types in a secret word while the other is not watching. Then the other player tries to guess the word. After guessing 10 wrong letters, the game is over and the man is hung.

PROGRAM STRUCTURE

```
      Get the secret word
GUESS Print the number of letters in the word.
      Get the letter guessed
      If the letter is in the word
           Put every occurence into
           the right place in A$
      Otherwise, G = G + 1
      Print G parts of the man being hung
           Print A$
      If the man is hung, or the word guessed
           Start a new game
      Otherwise, goto GUESS
```

The variable G contains the number of wrong guesses so far. To begin with, only subroutine 500, which does nothing, is executed. After that, for every wrong guess, one more of the subroutines is executed. Each prints another part of the man being hung.

A$ contains the word guessed so far. G$ is the letter guessed this time.

HANGMAN:

```
100 PRINT "NEW SECRET WORD?"
```

```
110 INPUT X$
120 LET W= LEN X$
130 DIM A$(W)
140 LET G=0
150 PRINT W;" LETTERS"
160 PRINT "GUESS?"
170 INPUT G$
180 CLS
190 LET C=0
200 FOR L=1 TO W
210 IF X$(L)=G$ THEN LET A$(L)=G$
220 IF A$(L)=G$ THEN LET C=1
230 NEXT L
240 IF NOT C THEN LET G=G+1
250 IF A$=X$ THEN PRINT "**YES**"
260 PRINT A$
270 PRINT
280 FOR L=500 TO 500+20*G STEP 20
290 GOSUB L
300 NEXT L
310 IF A$=X$ OR G=10 THEN RUN
320 PRINT
330 GOTO 150
500 RETURN
520 PRINT "▒▒▒"; (graphics A,A,A)
530 RETURN
540 PRINT "▒▒▒"  (graphics A,A,A)
550 RETURN
560 PRINT "△△▌"  (space,space,graphics 5)
570 RETURN
580 PRINT "△△▌"  (space,space,graphics 5)
590 RETURN
600 PRINT "△▀▀▌" (space,graphics E,E,5)
610 RETURN
620 PRINT "△▜";  (space,graphics R)
630 RETURN
640 PRINT "▜▘"   (graphics R,1)
650 RETURN
660 PRINT "△█ "  (space,graphics 8,space)
670 RETURN
680 PRINT "△▟";  (space,graphics Q)
```

```
690 RETURN
700 PRINT "▙"   (graphics 8,4)
710 RETURN
```

RUNNING THE PROGRAM

The word appears on the screen as you type it in, so make sure your opponent doesn't sneak a look. The computer does not check that the word is legal or contains only legal characters, but I don't think your opponent will be too pleased if it illegal.

When guessing you can only guess one letter at a time. As you guess wrong letters, a man being hung is drawn. The aim is to guess the word before the man is hung.

The letters you have guessed correctly are displayed in their correct positions at the top of the screen. You will be told how many letters are in the word.

QUADRATIC EQUATIONS

(c) by Neil Streeter

This program will solve equationss of the form

A*(X**2) + B*X + C = 0

for you. You enter the values of A,B and C. The program will solve for real or imaginary roots.

PROGRAM STRUCTURE

The program uses the formulae

X = (-B + SQR(B**2 - 4*A*C))/2*A
and X = (-B - SQR(B**2 - 4*A*C))/2*A

to calculate the roots of the equation.

If B**2 - 4*A*C is negative, then the roots are imaginary.

QUADRATIC EQUATIONS:

```
110 PRINT "A QUADRATIC EQUATION HAS",
      "THE FORM"
120 PRINT
130 PRINT"A (X)SQUARED + B (X) + C = 0"
140 PRINT
150 PRINT "INPUT A",
160 INPUT A
170 PRINT"A=";A
180 PRINT"INPUT B",
190 INPUT B
200 PRINT"B=";B
210 PRINT"INPUT C"
220 INPUT C
```

```
230 PRINT"C=";C
235 LET J=(ABS B)**2-(4*A*C)
240 IF J<0 THEN GOTO 500
250 LET P=SQR J
260 PRINT"THE ROOTS ARE REAL"
270 PRINT
280 PRINT"X=";(-B+P)/(2*A);
      " OR ";(-B-P)/(2*A)
290 STOP
500 PRINT"THE ROOTS ARE IMAGINARY"
510 PRINT
520 LET P=ABS J
530 PRINT"X=";-B/(2*A);" +/- ";
      (SQR P)/(2*A);"I"
540 PRINT
550 PRINT"WHERE I = THE SQUARE ROOT",
      "OF -1"
```

SIMULTANEOUS EQUATIONS

This program solves two simultaneous equations of the type

A*X + B*Y + C =0

You enter, in order, A,B and C for the first equation, then for the second.

If there is no solution, or there are an infinite number of solutions, you will be told that the problem is degenerate.

PROGRAM STRUCTURE

The input variables are stored in the array X A and B are the solutions.

D is the common denominator of the solutions.

Line 140 generates the A,B and C that appear down the screen as prompts as you input the data. 37 is one less than the code for A. So for I = 1 or 4, it prints A; for I = 2 or 5, B; and for I = 3 or 6, C.

```
100 DIM X(6)
110 PRINT "SOLUTIONS TO 2 EQUATIONS:"
120 PRINT "A*X + B*Y + C =0",,,"ENTER
       DATA"
130 FOR I=1 TO 6
140 PRINT CHR$ (37+I-INT ((I-1)/3)*3),
150 INPUT X(I)
160 PRINT X(I)
170 NEXT I
300 LET D = X(2)*X(4)-X(1)*X(5)
```

```
310 IF D = 0 THEN GOTO 360
320 LET A = ( X(3)*X(5) - X(2)*X(6) ) / D
330 LET B = ( X(1)*X(6) - X(3)*X(4) ) / D
340 PRINT "SOLUTIONS ARE:" , ,
     "X=" ; A , , "Y=" ; B
350 STOP
360 PRINT "DEGENERATE: NO SOLUTIONS"
```

ARCADE GAMES

* STAR WARS
* LUNAR LANDER
* ASTEROIDS IN SPACE
* BOMBS AWAY
* U.F.O.
* BREAKOUT
* SPACE TAXI

STAR WARS

(c) by Neil Streeter

You are the rear gunner in a space craft defending the Mother Ship. Through your space port you can see the enemy trying to get through the defenses of the Imperial forces.

You quickly shift your gun sight to get the enemy within firing range, and blast away. GOT HIM!

But what's that? Another one? YES - have to get him as well. If you can ward off the repeated attacks for 3 minutes you know that the Imperial forces will have been able to smash the enemy's power supply.

How many of the invaders can you destroy?

PROGRAM STRUCTURE

Lines 140 to 170 both print the space ship at its present location and blank out its previous position.

Since it can only move one space at a time, by writing blanks to all adjacent positions, the previous ship is overwritten.

```
100 LET A=600
110 LET B=0
120 LET H=INT (RND * 18)
130 LET V=INT (RND * 26)
140 PRINT AT H-1,V+1 ; "ΔΔ"
                (2 blanks)
150 PRINT AT H,V ; "Δ▀█▀Δ"
                (blank, graphics 2,T,blank)
```

```
160 PRINT AT H+1,V ; "△■■△"
              (blank, 2*graphic 2,blank)
170 PRINT AT H+2,V+1 ; "△△" (2 blanks)
180 PRINT AT 11,15 ; "+"
190 LET A=A-1
200 IF A=0 THEN GOTO 300
210 IF INKEY$="5" THEN LET V=V-1
220 IF INKEY$="6" THEN LET H=H+1
230 IF INKEY$="7" THEN LET H=H-1
240 IF INKEY$="8" THEN LET V=V+1
250 IF INKEY$="9" THEN GOTO 270
260 GOTO 140
270 IF H >= 10 AND H <= 11 AND V >= 13
      AND V <= 14 THEN LET B=B+1
280 CLS
290 GOTO 120
300 PRINT AT 0,0 ; "SCORE=" ; B
```

RUNNING THE PROGRAM:

The aim of this game is to shoot as many alien space ships as you can in the allotted time.

You can move the gun sight of your space ship with the buttons 5 to 8. They move the laser gun in the direction of the arrows. When the alien space ship is in the cross lines of your gun (the '+' in the centre of the screen) you can fire by pressing 9.

At the end of your alloted time at the guns, your score will be displayed. Can you shoot more invaders the next time they attack?

LUNAR LANDER

============

(c) by Neil Streeter and Beam Software

In this ZX81 version of the classic arcade game, you have to land your space ship safely.

The control panel of your space craft is able to display the velocity relative to the ground, the height above the ground and the amount of fuel left. An inset displays your position above ground graphically.

Unfortunately your control panel is not able to show your acceleration, so you have to use some intuition to get a good landing.

Your initial velocity is upwards, and you are at a distance of 2000ft above the ground. (A positive velocity corresponds to upwards travel, and a negative velocity to downwards travel).

If your velocity is more than 100ft/sec when you reach the ground, your craft will not be able to withstand the impact and you will ** CRASH **.

You can alter your velocity by applying thrust, and deciding the duration of that thrust. If you run out of fuel your attempts to apply upwards thrust will be futile and you will no doubt crash as your craft accelerates to the ground.

PROGRAM VARIABLES

V is the velocity of the ship, and initially it is a random number between 0 and 500.

H = the height of the ship above the ground.
R = the fuel reserve.
F = the force (or thrust) upon the ship.
A = the acceleration.
T = the time for which the force will act.

PROGRAM STRUCTURE

The new velocity and height are calculated using the formulae:

```
        V = 2*A*T + V
and     H = H + A*T**2 + V*T
```

You may note from the formula A = F - 32 that the acceleration is that of the earth. This is a Lunar Lander that is coming back to earth!

Line 200 prints the lander. If its distance from the ground is more than 2000ft it is printed at 0,2, since (H (2000) is false and therefore has value 0. So the the value of the whole expression is 0. If (H (2000) is true (and has value 1) then the value of the expression is 20-H/100

LUNAR LANDER:

```
110 LET V=INT (RND * 500)
120 LET H=2000
130 LET R=6000
140 GOTO 260
150 PRINT AT 1,0;"THRUST (0-99)"
160 INPUT F
180 PRINT AT 1,0;"TIME (1-6)ΔΔΔ"
190 INPUT T
200 CLS
210 IF F*T>R/10 THEN LET F=R/(10*T)
220 LET R=R-F*T*10
230 LET A=F-32
```

```
240 LET H=A*T**2+V*T+H
250 LET V=2*A*T+V
260 PRINT,"MOON LANDER"
270 IF H<=0 THEN LET H=0
280 PRINT,"SPEED ";V
290 PRINT,"DIST ";INT H
295 PRINT,"FUEL ";R
300 PRINT AT (H<2000)*(20-H/100),2;"▟▙"
                         (graphics TY)
305 PRINT AT 21,1;"▄▄▄▄" (graphics 6666)
310 IF H>0 THEN GOTO 150
320 PRINT AT 5,0;"SCORE=";100+V
330 IF V<-100 THEN PRINT"CRASH"
360 IF 100+V>0 THEN PRINT"LANDED"
```

RUNNING THE PROGRAM:

This 1K version does not feature "real time" action of the lander. Rather you have to decide what thrust you are going to apply and for how long. The program then calculates your position as a result of that decision and you start again.

Note that the height and velocity of the Lander are determined by the laws of physics: the effect of acceleration varies as the square of the time. If you apply a thrust of 80 for 2 seconds the effect is going to be quite different to applying that thrust for 4 seconds!

Hints for happy landing:

Your craft is initially travelling with an upwards velocity, just like a tennis ball as it leaves the tennis racket - if no further force is applied, the ship is going to continue travelling upwards for a little time and then fall down to earth gently again.

Until you gain familiarity with the controls apply thrust for only short periods of time: this will mean you will probably run out of fuel in your first few games, but you can use this expertise to make perfect landings later.

If you find the program too easy, you can alter the initial amount of fuel in your Lunar Lander by altering line 130.

Best of luck, Lunar Man.

ASTEROIDS IN SPACE

(c) by Neil Streeter

You are travelling through space in your space ship, when you suddenly encounter a meteor storm.

You can steer your ship past these using your rudder controls only (key '5' to go left and '8' to go right) - hyperdrive has been disabled by one of the meteors.

As if this was not bad enough, if you do survive the meteor storm, you will find that you have become so disoriented that you are travelling the wrong way in the space lanes. All the other space ships are coming at you.

You must steer past these in the same way as before, but the ships are bigger than the meteors, so it is more difficult.

Eventually you will CRASH! When you do, you will find your survival rating on the screen of your spaceship console.

PROGRAM STRUCTURE

The program uses the SCROLL funtion to move the meteors and space ships (other than yours).

When the display is SCROLLed, your ship will move with everything else, so it is overwritten with blanks, then printed again in the correct position. In this way, your ship stays on the same line in the screen while everything else moves.

The positions of the meteors coming towards you are kept in A,B,C,D and E; with E being the closest. By comparing E with the position of your ship, the program determines whether or not you are about to crash.

ASTEROIDS:

```
100 LET A$="▨" (graphics A)
105 LET N=0
110 LET A=0
115 LET B=0
120 LET C=0
125 LET D=0
130 LET T=1
135 LET X=12
160 LET R=INT (RND*27)
170 PRINT AT 21,R;A$
180 SCROLL
190 SCROLL
200 LET N=N+T
205 IF N=100 THEN LET A$="▚▟"
              (graphics T4)
210 IF N=104 THEN LET T=2
215 LET E=D
220 LET D=C
230 LET C=B
240 LET B=A
250 LET A=R
255 PRINT AT 9,X-2;"△△△△△△" (6 spaces)
260 PRINT AT 11,X;"▛▜" (graphics YT)
270 IF X>=E-2 AND X<=E+T THEN GOTO 500
280 IF INKEY$="5" THEN LET X=X-T
290 IF INKEY$="8" THEN LET X=X+T
300 GOTO 160
500 PRINT AT 11,X-1;"CRASH"
510 PRINT AT 0,0;"SCORE=";N
```

BOMBS AWAY

(c) by Clifford Ramshaw

The aim of this game is to land your plane; but the runway is covered with rubble which you must clear away first.

Your plane moves right and descends slowly automatically, and you can drop bombs to clear away the rubble by typing 'F'. If there is any rubble left by the time your plane tries to land, you will CRASH; otherwise you will glide to a halt. (ED: We think so, but no-one here has been able to get a perfect score yet!!)

This is quite a difficult task, so good luck.

PROGRAM STRUCTURE

The only record of where there is rubble is in the display.

To find out if the plane is about to crash, the program PEEKs at addresses 16398 and 16399 which contain the address of the next location to be printed.

When we PEEK in memory we look to see what is in that particular memory location. We know from the ZX81 manual that memory locations 16398 and 16399 have been set aside by the operating system to hold the position in memory of the next position to be printed.

This is a little like the ability to specify where we want to print by using PRINT AT. In fact we can have the same effect as PRINT AT by

changing (ie. POKEing) the contents of 16398 and 16399. Of course it's much harder to do it that way so no-one does that, but there is no BASIC command which lets us say something like

```
IF PRINT AT = 137 THEN ...
```

Instead if we calculate

```
PEEK 16398 + 256 * PEEK 16399
```

we will get the address in memory of the next position to be printed.

This is not quite the same as knowing which line and position but it's enough for us to work out what is there. If we look at the contents of that position (ie. PEEK) - hence that horrible

```
PEEK ( PEEK etc.  )
```

in line 270 - we will know what is just ahead of the aeroplane.

There are three possibilities for what we will find just ahead of the plane: an empty space, an End-of-Line character, or rubble. This is what we check for in Line 270. If it's rubble, STOP!!!

The rest of the program is simple to follow - extremely ingenious and a great game.

BOMBS AWAY:

```
110 LET A=1
120 LET B=0
130 LET S=B
140 FOR I=B TO 19
150 PRINT AT 9,I;"▆" (graphic G)
160 PRINT AT 10,I;"▨" (graphic A)
170 NEXT I
180 PRINT AT A,B;"△" (space)
190 LET B=B+1
200 IF B<22 THEN GOTO 240
210 LET A=A+1
```

```
220 PRINT AT S,B-1;" " (space)
230 LET B=0
240 PRINT AT A,B;">"
250 IF A=9 AND B=19 THEN STOP
260 PRINT AT A,B+1;
270 IF PEEK (PEEK 16398 + 256*PEEK
      16399)=137 THEN STOP
280 IF S=0 THEN GOTO 400
290 PRINT AT S,B-1;" " (space)
300 IF S=9 THEN GOTO 340
310 LET S=S+1
320 PRINT AT S,B;"■" (graphic 3)
330 GOTO 180
340 LET S=0
400 IF INKEY$="F" THEN LET S=A
405 GOTO 180
```

RUNNING THE PROGRAM:

It will only take you a few games to realise that you need good aim to clear all the rubble!

The BOMBS AWAY is controlled by the FIRE button: the use of the INKEY$ routine in line 400 means that by pressing 'F' continuously you will keep on dropping bombs - but that's not good enough to clear the runway.

Like any good aircraft pilot, you need to exercise split second timing and sound judgement as to when to drop the Bomb.

U.F.O.
======

(c) by J. M. Revis

The aim of this game is to strike the fast-moving U.F.O. as it flies overhead.

It is essential to be accurate - those U.F.O.s will keep trying to invade the earth until they are eventually destroyed.

PROGRAM STRUCTURE

The U.F.O. is printed by two FOR-NEXT loops. One prints it going from left to right; then the other prints it from right to left. The U.F.O. is printed, then immediately overwritten with blanks.

It is by using the shortest possible number of instructions in the FOR-NEXT loops that the U.F.O. is able to move so fast. Unfortunately this also causes the image of the U.F.O. to flicker.

The function INKEY$ is used to input the 'fire' command. Unlike the INPUT statement, INKEY$ doesn't wait for input from the keyboard, so if you don't type 'F' the program keeps going.

U.F.O.:

```
105 LET B=2
110 FOR N=30 TO 1 STEP -1
120 PRINT AT B,N;"▄▀▄" (graphics T,Y)
```

```
140 PRINT AT B,N;"ΔΔ" (2 spaces)
145 IF INKEY$="F" THEN GOTO 205
150 NEXT N
160 FOR N= 1 TO 30
170 PRINT AT B,N;"▄█▄" (graphics TY)
180 PRINT AT B,N;"ΔΔ" (2 spaces)
185 IF INKEY$="F" THEN GOTO 205
190 NEXT N
200 GOTO 110
205 PRINT AT B,N;"▄█▄" (graphics TY)
210 FOR X=20 TO 1 STEP -1
212 LET Y=15
215 PRINT AT X,Y;"▄█▄ " (graphics T4)
220 PRINT AT X,Y;"ΔΔ" (2 spaces)
222 IF B=X AND Y=N THEN GOTO 230
225 NEXT X
227 GOTO 40
230 PRINT AT X,Y;"BOOOOM"
```

BREAKOUT

(c) by Clifford Ramshaw

This program is a BASIC version of the TV game variously known as BREAKOUT or BRICK WALL.

Although a machine language version of this game is quite easily done in 1K it is a remarkable achievement by Clifford Ramshaw to have managed to give us a BASIC version which fits into 1K.

The aim of this game is to knock out as much of the wall as possible. You keep the ball in the court by moving your paddle left (with the 'Z' key) or right (with the 'M' key) to hit the ball.

To make the game more interesting, the angle at which the ball bounces back is random.

PROGRAM STRUCTURE

X and Y are the coordinates of the ball. DX and DY give the gradient of the path of the ball. The ball is moved by adding DX to X, and DY to Y then plotting the new position. The old position is cleared with the UNPLOT function. If this position is part of the wall, then there will be a hole in the wall.

BREAKOUT:

```
105  GOSUB 1000
110  LET P=10
115  LET X=P
120  LET Y=21
```

```
125  LET DX=1
130  LET DY=DX
135  UNPLOT X,Y
140  LET X=X+DX
145  LET Y=Y+DY
150  PLOT X,Y
152  IF Y>42 THEN LET DX= INT (RND*3 -1)
155  IF Y>42 THEN LET DY=-DY
160  IF X<3 OR X>22 THEN LET DX=-DX
165  IF Y>19 THEN GOTO 180
170  IF X<>P AND X<>P+1 THEN STOP
175  LET DY=-DY
180  UNPLOT P,19
185  UNPLOT P+1,19
190  IF INKEY$="X" THEN LET P=P-1
195  IF INKEY$="M" THEN LET P=P+1
200  PLOT P,19
205  PLOT P+1,19
210  GOTO 135
1000 FOR I=1 TO 13
1005 PRINT"▒"; (graphic A)
1010 NEXT I
1015 FOR I=0 TO 11
1020 PRINT AT I,0;"█" (graphic space)
1025 PRINT AT I,13;"█" (graphic space)
1030 NEXT I
1035 RETURN
```

RUNNING THE PROGRAM:

After you press (RUN) (NEW LINE), you will see the two boundary walls of the court being drawn up, and then the row of bricks across the back wall.

Your paddle is 2 characters wide across the bottom of the court area, and you must position it correctly to catch the ball as it comes towards the baseline.

If you should miss the program will STOP. Press (RUN) (NEW LINE) for a new game.

This one is a real challenge.

If you want to make it much easier and allow yourself an unlimited number of balls to knock the wall down, you can change line 300 to read:

```
300  IF X <> P AND X <> P+1 THEN RUN 40
```

This will have the effect of leaving the old ball and paddle on the baseline, but as you play on they will be erased.

SPACE TAXI

(c) by Clifford Ramshaw

Space taxi is a game in which you are in a space ship and you must fly over the white mountains, dodging the obstacles for as long as possible.

You move the space ship up (using the 'Z' key) or down (using the 'M' key), but the movement to the right is automatic.

If your ship collides with the mountains or an obstacle, your score is shown and a new game started. If the ship reaches the right hand side safely, it will reappear on the left with a new display.

PROGRAM STRUCTURE:

The subroutine at 1000 sets up the mountains and the obstacles. The height of the mountains, and the position of the obstacles is random. They are shown on the screen, and this is the only record of where they are. Line 170 looks at the next position to be printed, and checks whether or not it is blank.

The position of the space ship is recorded by co-ordinates X and Y. Lines 80 and 90 control the vertical movement of the space ship, and the X component is automatically incremented.

SPACE TAXI:

```
10   LET S=0
20   LET Y=1
```

```
30   LET X=0
40   CLS
50   GOSUB 1000
60   PRINT AT Y,X;"█" (graphic space)
70   LET D=0
80   IF INKEY$="M" THEN LET D=-1
90   IF INKEY$="Z" THEN LET D=1
100  LET S=S+1
110  LET X=X+1
120  IF X=31 THEN GOTO 30
130  LET Y=Y+D
140  IF Y<0 THEN LET Y=0
150  PRINT AT Y,X;">"  (graphic greater than)
160  PRINT AT Y,X+1;
170  IF PEEK (PEEK 16398 + 256 * PEEK 16399)<>0
       THEN GOTO 60
180  PRINT S
190  PAUSE 100
200  RUN
1000 FOR J=0 TO 31
1005 FOR I=0 TO 2+INT(RND*3)
1010 PRINT AT I,J;"█"  (graphic space)
1015 NEXT I
1020 NEXT J
1025 FOR I=1 TO 15
1030 PRINT AT INT(RND*5),INT(RND*27)+5;" "
                             (space)
1035 NEXT I
1040 RETURN
```

RUNNING THE PROGRAM:

As you can see, this is only a short program but exceptionally well designed and great fun to play. Moreover it has a great scoring routine which gives you a score as soon as you crash.

If you manage to get through all the obstacles on your first pass through the mountains, another mountain range appears and the score is

continually updated.

You will note that Line 200 contains the instruction (RUN) which you would not normally expect to find in a program listing.

This is a device to enable continuous running of the program: if you should happen to CRASH, then the score will be displayed for some seconds, and then the game starts over again. In effect this saves you the need from having to type (RUN) (NEW LINE) at the end of each pass through the mountains.

Watch out: Space Taxi is addictive!

ZX 81 UTILITY PROGRAMS

* BUBBLE SORT

* LINE RENUMBERING

* MACHINE CODE EDITOR

BUBBLE SORT

This program sorts 15 numbers. You can watch the smallest numbers 'bubble' to the top on the screen. If you don't want to input your own numbers, the computer will generate them for you.

PROGRAM STRUCTURE

This program would probably be more useful as a subroutine than by itself. You could use it, for example, to order the cards in a hand in a Bridge program, for example. Nonetheless it is an interesting program in its own right.

If you want to use it as a subroutine, note:

The variable N contains the number of items to be sorted. If this is not 15, then change line 100.

The numbers to be sorted are in array P. If your program sets up the array, then all you need to sort the array are lines 270 to 380.

Lines 350 and 360 just print the array so that you can watch the sort. You may want to delete them if you are using the sort in another program.

100-110 INITIALIZATION
120-190 ENTER NUMBERS FROM KEYBOARD
200-220 COMPUTER GENERATED NUMBERS
230-260 PRINT NUMBERS
270-380 SORT

The program works by comparing two elements in the array (in line 310) and changing their order if necessary.

It is called a Bubble Sort because the "lighter" numbers seem to "bubble" to the top. When there are no more bubbles, the program stops.

BUBBLE SORT DEMONSTRATION:

```
100 LET N=15
110 DIM P(N)
120 PRINT "OWN NUMBERS?"
130 INPUT B$
140 IF B$="N" THEN GOTO 200
150 PRINT "ENTER 15 NUMBERS"
160 FOR Y=1 TO N
170 INPUT P(Y)
180 NEXT Y
190 GOTO 230
200 FOR X=1 TO N
210 LET P(X)=15*RND+1
220 NEXT X
230 CLS
240 FOR X=1 TO N
250 PRINT AT X,0;P(X)
260 NEXT X
270 FOR J=1 TO N-1
280 LET K=J+1
290 FOR I=K TO N
300 LET L=N+K-I
310 IF P(L)>P(J) THEN GOTO 370
320 LET T=P(L)
330 LET P(L)=P(J)
340 LET P(J)=T
350 PRINT AT J,0;P(J);"△△"
360 PRINT AT L,0;P(L);"△△"
370 NEXT I
380 NEXT J
```

RUNNING THE PROGRAM:

This program gives a very nice visual

demonstration of the sorting process, so it is much more interesting if run in the SLOW mode. If you are going to be loading this program from cassette, be sure to change back to SLOW before pressing RUN.

The program will ask you if you would like to submit your own disordered numbers or let the computer choose its own (line 140).

Then just sit back and watch the program at work.

LINE RENUMBERING

This is a program that you may find useful if you are in the habit of developing programs and find yourself at the end of the day with oddly numbered lines and no room to fit in that last brilliantly conceived routine in the middle.

Enter this short program, type (RUN 9990), (NEW LINE), and next time you look at the listing, just like magic it has all been cleaned up.

An added bonus is that at the cost of only one more line you can have a screen display of all lines which contain a GOTO or GOSUB statement.

(Because the ZX81 allows computed GOTOs and GOSUBs as in GOTO 100 + A*10 it is not possible for a program to renumber the GOTOs and GOSUBs - but at least you'll know where they are and won't miss any).

TEST PROGRAM:

The following program is a 'test' program in that it won't change any of the lines numbers but will illustrate the operation of the Line Renumbering Program.

The program assumes that the first line in your program is numbered 100 and that you want the program lines to increase in steps of 10. To change this, alter line 9990 to change the starting line number and line 9998 to change the size of the increment.

You cannot LOAD a program from tape once you

already have a program in memory, so either load this program first whenever you are going to develop programs or key it in as required - it's only short, anyway.

```
9990  LET L = 110
9991  FOR N = 16515 TO 17400       (assumes 1K.
           Change to '16515 TO 32700' for 16K)
9993  IF PEEK N <> 118 THEN GOTO 9999
9994  IF PEEK (N+1) > 38 THEN STOP
9995  PRINT 256 * PEEK (N+1) + PEEK (N+2);
        "△ ->";      (space, minus, greater than)
9996  PRINT L
9997  LET N = N + 3 + PEEK (N+3) +
        256 * PEEK (N+4)
9998  LET L = L + 10
9999  NEXT N
```

If you add a short program of oddly numbered lines you will be able to test this test program.

Enter (RUN 9990) (NEW LINE) and the screen display will show you the old line numbers and what they would be converted to if they were renumbered.

LINE RENUMBERING MODEL 1:

The Line Renumbering Program is identical to the test program above, but we replace lines 9995 and 9996 as follows:

```
9995  POKE N+1, INT (L / 256)
9996  POKE N+2, L - 256 * INT (L / 256)
```

The program will now do the renumbering that was only indicated in the test program. Note that the screen display will now not be shown.

This program occupies about 260 bytes of memory.

If you are concerned about memory usage, see "Machine Code Editor" where a 38 byte version of this program can be found.

LINE RENUMBERING MODEL 2:

The Super deluxe Line Renumbering Program is as follows:

```
9990  LET L = 100
9991  LET N = 16509
9992  IF PEEK N > 38 THEN STOP
9993  POKE N, INT (L/256)
9994  POKE N+1, L - 256 * INT (L/256)
9995  FOR N = N + 4 TO N + 3 + PEEK (N+2) +
        256 * PEEK (N+3)
9996  IF PEEK N = 236 OR PEEK N = 237 THEN
        PRINT L; "-" ; CHR$ PEEK N
9997  NEXT N
9998  LET L = L + 10
9999  GOTO 9992
```

Your screen will now show the line number of all GOTOs and GOSUBs. If you are using a line increment different from 10 then don't forget to make the appropriate changes in this line.

The Model 2 Line Renumbering Program requires about 310 bytes.

The "Show Only" version can be obtained by replacing lines 9993 and 9994 by:

```
        9993 PRINT 256 * PEEK N + PEEK (N+1);
                " → " ; L
```

Note to shorten the programs:

You will no doubt have noticed that line 9997 is quite cumbersome.

That line actually serves two purposes:

1. To determine where the start of the next BASIC is, and
2. To eliminate the possibility of finding an End-of-Line character in the middle of line.

The latter is possible without your even knowing about it because of the way the ZX 81 treats numbers in a BASIC line - it converts them to 6-byte code for numbers.

This means that an innocuous number like 123 actually ends up containing the dreaded End-of-Line character in it!

You can shorten line 9997 to read

```
9997 LET N = N + 4
```

at the risk of a slower program and of finding an end of line character in the text.

Should this happen, most of the time no problem will arise except lines after the offending one will not be renumbered and occasionally your number will be corrupted.

The "Show Only" version of Line Renumbering will show you when that happens.

Just a tip if you are tight on memory and forgot to enter the machine code version first!

A super deluxe "short" Line Renumbering Program is possible with the addition of the following line:

```
9992 IF PEEK N = 236 OR PEEK N = 237 THEN
     PRINT L-10; "=" ; CHR$ PEEK N
```

MACHINE CODE EDITOR

The aim of this short BASIC program is to enable you to enter a machine code program into a REMark statement at the beginning of the program. Incidentally, this program will also illustrate the uses of PEEKs and POKEs.

The first line of the program is numbered line 100 and is a REMark statement containing 32 number '1's: this is where we will place the machine code, and as far as we are concerned, it could be filled with the letters of the alphabet or any 32 graphics characters. All that this line does is to reserve 32 bytes of memory at an address we know. (The ZX81 manual tells us that the first byte of the REM statement will be at memory location 16514: you could check this out writing a short program to PEEK around memory!)

The subroutine located at lines 500 onwards PEEKs at what is in the Ith location (I = 0 to 31 in this case, but if you want to enter longer machine code programs, you could alter this maximum value of I in line 120. Be sure to make the REM statement long enough).

To PEEK at a memory location is merely to look at what is in there. The subroutine on its return contains the contents of that memory location in A$.

You then have a choice of leaving that memory location as it is (Press (ENTER) which makes A$ = "" - see line 170) or of entering what you would like the memory location to contain. Your input has to be in 2 digit Hex code.

Line 190 POKEs what you decided you wanted in to that memory location. POKE is computer for PUT - we are therefore only putting a selected value into that space.

MACHINE CODE EDITOR:

```
100  REM 11111111111111111111111111111111
                    (32 times '1')
110  LET S = 16514
120  FOR I = 0 TO 31
130  SCROLL
140  GOSUB 500
150  PRINT I ; "=" ; A$ ; ". -) .";
160  INPUT A$
170  IF A$ = "" THEN GOTO 200
180  LET V = 16 * CODE A$ + CODE A$ (2) - 476
190  POKE S+I, V
200  GOSUB 500
210  PRINT A$
220  NEXT I
230  STOP
500  LET V = PEEK (S+I)
510  LET H = INT (V / 16)
520  LET L = V - 16 * H
530  LET A$ = CHR$ (H + 28) + CHR$ (L + 28)
540  RETURN
```

RUNNING THE PROGRAM Part 1:

When you have entered (RUN) (NEW LINE) the screen will display the following at the bottom:

```
    0 = 1D  -)
```

and the cursor will indicate it is waiting for a string input.

What the display is showing you is that the contents of the 0th location is 1D (in hex: you can confirm this is the number '1' by checking

the table at the back of the ZX81 manual).

If you now enter 1E (NEW LINE), you will see

```
    0 = 1D  -)  1E
    1 = 1D  -)
```

This means that the contents of the 0th location were changed from 1D to 1E.

Enter the values 1E, 1F, 20, 21, 22, 23, 24, 25, 26, 27, 28, 29, 2A, 2B, 2C, 2D, 2E, 2F, 30, 31, 32, 33, 34, 35, 36, 37, 38, 39, 3A, 3B, 3C, 3D.

If you now look at the listing of the program you will see that we changed the contents of the REM line! It now reads

```
100 REM 23456789ABCDEFGHIJKLMNOPQRSTUVWX
```

This should be a pretty good demonstration of what PEEK and POKE is all about. Obviously we can also PEEK or POKE into the screen area, the variables held in memory, and so on.

RUNNING THE PROGRAM Part 2:

We will now use the same program to enter a 32 byte machine language routine which can renumber the lines for us. This is similar to our program LINE RENUMBERING except it is not able to indicate which lines contain GOTOs and GOSUBs.

The benefits of this machine language routine however are that it is much faster in execution and that it occupies less memory that the BASIC listing of our other program.

Enter the following values:
11, A2, 40, 21, 64, 00, 1A, 3D, FE, 75, C0, 13, 1A, FE, 27, D0, 01, 0A, 00, 09, EB, 72, 23, 73,

23, 4E, 23, 46, 09, EB, 18, E6.

You can now test this machine language program by entering the line (without line number)

    PRINT USR 16514 (NEW LINE)

If you now look at the listing you will see that the lines have all been renumbered! (If you want the BASIC program to still work, alter lines 140 and 200 to now read GOSUB 240).

It is beyond the scope of this book to explain how the machine code works, but for the benefit of readers who understand machine language we have included the assembly listing with comments.

If you do not understand machine language, we recommend our book 'Machine Language Programming Made Simple - see details at the end of the book for price and ordering details.

The routine you now have stored in Line 100 will work for any program. Just delete line 110 onwards, and press (CLEAR) (NEW LINE). You now have a short program (38 bytes) which will renumber lines for you just by entering

    PRINT USR 16514 (NEW) LINE)

Save this program on cassette and load it every time you want to develop your own programs. When you have finished developing your program, you can delete line 100 and replace it by a REM statement with the name of your program, such as

    100 REM THE GREATEST PROGRAM EVER

or some other suitable title.

RUNNING THE PROGRAM Part 3:

We can use the same program to also create any other machine language program we may find useful.

For example, it is possible to write a 13 byte machine language program which will tell you to the byte how much memory you have left. This 'Memory Left' utility can even be used during the running of a program!

Because we have a shorter machine language program, set up line 100 to have only 13 number '1's, and amend line 120 to read

```
    100  FOR I = 0 TO 12
```

Enter the following values into the program when requested to do so:

B7, ED, 5B, 1C, 40, ED, 62, 39, ED, 52, E5, C1, C9.

This short machine code program will return the memory left in answer to entering PRINT USR 16514. Try this now. Now delete all lines except for line 100 and press (CLEAR) NEW LINE). (This will remove all the variables created in rinning the machine code editor program). See what the result of PRINT USR 16514 is now.

As mentioned above, this utility can even be used during the running of a program, as in the following line:

```
    IF USR 16514 ( 50 THEN STOP
```

This can be very useful in a developing programs, and so on.

The assembler codes for this short machine language program are:

```
B7              OR   A
ED 5B 1C 40     LD   DE, (16412)
ED 62           SBC  HL, HL
39              ADD  HL, SP
ED 52           SBC  HL, DE
```

```
E5          PUSH HL
C1          POP  BC
C9          RET
```

It is beyond the scope of this book to talk about machine language programming, but it should be obvious from these few examples that machine language programming is able to provide many benefits for users of the Sinclair ZX81.

The line renumbering routine, for example, is able to be reduce from some 260 bytes to only 38 bytes and will even execute much more quickly. The Memory Left utility, for example, cannot be properly duplicated in a BASIC program because it is impossible to determine how far down the stack is without recourse to machine language.

If you are interested in learning machine language, we recommend our book, MACHINE LANGUAGE PROGRAMMING MADE SIMPLE. Price and ordering details are available at the back of this book.

You may be interested to know that both the Line Renumbering and Memory Left utilities can be combined in one REM statement if you so desire. Set Line 100 to have 45 number '1's in it, and amend line 120 to read FOR I = 0 TO 44. Enter the Memory Left code first, then the Line Renumbering code. (The code is exactly the same EXCEPT for the second entry in the Line Renumbering Program: change from A2 to AF).

To obtain Memory Left, use PRINT USR 16514, while to obtain Line Renumbering use PRINT USR 16527.

RUNNING THE PROGRAM Part 4:

It is not necessary to only store machine code routines in the REM statement. You can use this

program to store any numbers as long as they are in the range 0 to 255.

There may be times when you need to store a lot of variables for one of your own programs, but don't want to store them in a variable because this would use up 6 bytes per number.

This program is ideal for that kind of situation. We use this principle in the program 'Doctor ZX81'.

```
                ;       ZX81 LINE RENUMBERING ROUTINE
                ;
                ;       CODE TO BE STORED IN REM STATEMENT
                ;       NUMBERED AS LINE 100
                ;       NOTE: THIS MUST BE FIRST LINE OF PROGRAM
                ;
                ;
4082                    ORG     16514
                ;
                ;DEFINE STARTING POSITION AS END OF REM LINE 100
4082 11A240     START   LD      DE,16546        ;END OF REM LINE 100
4085 216400             LD      HL,100          ;LINE # OF FIRST LINE
                ;
                ;CHECK WE HAVE AN END-OF-LINE CHARACTER
4088 1A         ENDLIN  LD      A,(DE)          ;CHECK LOCATION CONTAI
4089 3D                 DEC     A               ; END OF LINE CHARACTE
408A FE75               CP      75H             ;IF A=75H, ALL OK
408C C0                 RET     NZ              ;OTHERWISE ABORT
                ;
                ;DE POINTS TO NEW LINE START
                ;HL CONTAINS LINE # OF PREVIOUS LINE
408D 13         NXTLIN  INC     DE      ;DE POINTS TO NUMBER OF LINE
408E 1A                 LD      A,(DE)  ;CHECK IF LINE # ) 9999
408F FE27               CP      27H     ;IF YES, ALL LINES RENUMBERED
4091 D0                 RET     NC      ; SO ALL FINISHED
                ;
4092 010A00             LD      BC,10   ;THIS IS LINE INCREMENT
4095 09                 ADD     HL,BC   ;CALCULATE NEW LINE #
                ;
                ;INSERT NEW LINE # IN MEMORY
4096 EB                 EX      DE,HL   ;SWAP HL,DE
4097 72                 LD      (HL),D  ; SO THE DE HAS LINE #
4098 23                 INC     HL      ;POKE MEMORY WITH
4099 73                 LD      (HL),E  ; NEW LINE NUMBER
                ;
                ;GET LINE LENGTH AND SKIP TO END OF LINE
409A 23                 INC     HL      ;HL NOW POINTS TO
409B 4E                 LD      C,(HL)  ; LENGTH OF LINE
409C 23                 INC     HL      ;LOAD BC WITH LINE LENGTH
409D 46                 LD      B,(HL)
409E 09                 ADD     HL,BC   ;HL NOW POINTS TO END OF LINE
                ;
409F EB                 EX      DE,HL   ;SWAP HL,DE TO RESTORE
                                        ; ORIGINAL CONDITIONS
40A0 18E6               JR      ENDLIN  ;RENUMBER NEXT LINE
```

CHALLENGING THE ZX 81 : 1K

* MASTERMIND
* DOCTOR ZX 81
* CAVES AND PITFALLS
* DRAUGHTS

MASTERMIND

In this game, the computer generates a number of as many digits as you specify (between 3 and 7).

You then have to try to guess the number.

After each guess, the computer will tell you how many of the digits you entered were in its number, and how many were in the correct position. There are no repeated digits in the number chosen by the computer. This means that it will never come up with a number such as 1231.

When you work out what the number is, your score will be displayed. If you get frustrated, and want to give up, type NEWLINE when you are asked for a number. Of course, in that case you'll never find out what the number was.

PROGRAM STRUCTURE

The computer's number is stored as an array of digits in A.

Your number is stored as a string of characters in B$. The function CODE used in line 380 returns the numerical code for the first character in the string. '28' is the code for '0', so CODE(B$)-28 gives the numerical value of the first character in B$.

C contains the number of digits in the correct position.
R contains the number of digits that are in the computer's number.

MASTERMIND:

```
100 PRINT "WELCOME TO MASTERMIND"
110 PRINT "ENTER NO OF DIGITS
      IN NUMBER (3-7)"
120 INPUT N
130 DIM A(N)
200 FOR I=1 TO N
210 LET X= INT (RND*10)
220 FOR J=1 TO I
230 IF X=A(J) THEN GOTO 210
240 NEXT J
250 LET A(I)=X
260 NEXT I
270 LET G=0
280 GOTO 530
300 INPUT B$
310 IF B$="" THEN STOP
320 CLS
330 PRINT B$
340 LET R=0
350 LET C=R
360 LET G=G+1
370 FOR I=1 TO N
380 LET X=CODE(B$)-28
390 IF X=A(I) THEN LET C=C+1
400 FOR J=1 TO N
410 IF X=A(J) THEN LET R=R+1
420 NEXT J
430 LET B$=B$(2 TO )
440 NEXT I
450 IF C=N THEN GOTO 600
500 PRINT "NUMBERS RIGHT=";R
510 PRINT "CORRECT POSITIONS=";C
520 PRINT
530 PRINT "ENTERΔ";N;"ΔFIGURE GUESS"
540 GOTO 300
600 PRINT "YOU DID IT INΔ";G;"ΔGUESSES"
```

DOCTOR ZX 81

In this program we will try to bring within the limitations of a 1K machine a conversational program. This is the beginning of a program which shows the possibilities of Artificial Intelligence in the Sinclair ZX 81.

Unfortunately because of the restrictions of memory, Doctor ZX 81 is not a very stimulating conversationalist.

In fact, some people say that like most professionals, he doesn't seem to listen to what ordinary people like you and me have to say!

STRUCTURE OF THE PROGRAM:

In this program we will have a conversational exchange between the computer and a 'patient'. We will have to define the vocabulary of the good Doctor and the sentences he will speak.

In order to fit all this into 1K we have divided up the program into three smaller programs: one to define the vocabulary, one to define the sentences, and the last one to make the Doctor talk to us.

Vocabulary:

We will define the vocabulary into a string variable called A$. This is what Program 2 does.

The point to remember is that it is not essential to keep the string variable in the program

listing as well as in memory. Thus after we have (RUN) Program 2, we can delete the string variable A$ from the program listing and still have it available for Program 3.

The string variable consists of 38 words which we define as the Doctor's vocabulary. By defining the vocabulary in this way, we can then refer to any word by its position in A$ and not have to waste memory by using the full word many times.

We put a space after each word and that is the way we will be able to tell where each word ends.

SENTENCES FOR THE DOCTOR:

After we defined the vocabulary for the Doctor we noticed that the length of that vocabulary was less that 256 characters (in fact only 203).

You can immediately see that if 38 words require 203 bytes we need to conserve memory wherever we can.

Since each word can thus be defined by a single number between 1 and 203 (and thus would need only 1 byte in memory in an ideal system), it seems a waste of memory to use a normal variable for each word which takes up 6 bytes!.

We want to define 11 sentences with a total of 75 words: using normal variables would be counterproductive as we would run out of memory!

Instead we will use a REM statement at the beginning of the program to store the words we want to use in our sentences. We will use a simple BASIC program to POKE the numbers we want in to the REM statement.

If you have problems understanding what POKE and PEEK is all about, have a look at the program "Machine Code Editor" which may make it clearer to you.

As no word can start at location 0, we will use '0' to define the end of a sentence in much the same way that we used a space to define the end of a word.

CONVERSING WITH THE DOCTOR:

This is Program 3. By the time we come to run this program we have the vocabulary stored in A$ in memory (and so cannot use (RUN) or (CLEAR)) and the sentences in the REM statement in line 100.

The program consists of taking each word in turn (variable I) and displaying each character of that word (variable J). If the character about to be displayed is a space, we then go to the next word (Line 170 and 180).

If the word about to be displayed is word # 0, than we know the sentence is finished and we display a question and wait for the user's response.

DOCTOR ZX 81:

Program 1:

This program defines the sentences we will be showing on the screen and stores the word numbers in the REM statement defined in Line 100.

```
100  REM 11111111111111111111111111
```

```
   1111112222222222222222222222222
   2222223333333333333333333333333
   3                (at least 90 chars)
110  FOR I = 1 TO 89
120  SCROLL
130  PRINT AT 1,1 ; I ; " ▲ ▲ ";
140  INPUT V$
150  IF V$ = "" THEN GOTO 180
160  PRINT V$
170  POKE 16513 + I, VAL V$
180  NEXT I
```

Press (RUN) (NEW LINE). Enter the following numbers followed by (NEW LINE) when each value of the word number is shown:

    1 68 (NEW LINE)
    2 141 etc..

1 = 68	21 = 36	41 = 0	61 = 85	81 =158
2 =141	22 =195	42 = 36	62 =102	82 = 27
3 = 88	23 = 46	43 =199	63 = 0	83 = 74
4 =199	24 =161	44 = 60	64 = 36	84 = 14
5 =131	25 = 0	45 = 51	65 =199	85 = 0
6 =175	26 = 36	46 =153	66 = 60	86 =124
7 = 85	27 =195	47 = 3	67 = 51	87 =109
8 =199	28 =147	48 = 0	68 =153	88 = 20
9 = 97	29 =153	49 = 36	69 = 3	89 = 0
10 = 0	30 = 85	50 =195	70 = 0	
11 =175	31 =109	51 = 27	71 = 83	
12 = 32	32 = 0	52 = 74	72 =147	
13 =195	33 =185	53 =158	73 =124	
14 =120	34 = 36	54 = 51	74 = 39	
15 =199	35 =195	55 = 60	75 = 56	
16 = 97	36 =147	56 = 0	76 =161	
17 =167	37 =195	57 = 36	77 =180	
18 = 14	38 = 46	58 =195	78 =189	
19 = 0	39 =153	59 =147	79 =195	
20 = 79	40 =171	60 =153	80 = 92	

After you have (RUN) this program, you will get a

surprise if you look at the listing of the program: Line 100 will be now be full of strange letters, commands and graphics chharacters. This is perfectly normal.

Delete all lines of Program 1 except for Line 100. You should now have a program listing that looks like

```
   100  REM  $ ? SIN  = J ? SIN ?  etc...
```

You can now also press (CLEAR) (NEW LINE) to delete the variables held in memory to make more room for the string variable you are about to enter in Program 2.

Program 2:

Add the following line 110 to the line 100 you already have:

```
110  LET A$ = "A ACCEPTABLE AGAIN BYEBYE COME DID
DO ENOUGH FEEL FIND FOR FRIENDS HELLO HERE HOW I
IS I/M LIKE NAME NORMAL REASONABLE SAY THAT/S
THERAPIST THERE THINK THIS TO TODAY WAS WAY WHAT
WHEN WHY WOULD YOU YOUR  "
```

Be sure that you leave a single space only after each word (including the last word).

It is important that each word should be spelt properly because if you have any errors, the words after that may not be printed out correctly.

Press (RUN) (NEW LINE). The variable A$ is now stored in memory, so let's check that there are no errors.

Enter the following lines without line numbers:
PRINT A$(1) (NEW LINE) - You should see A

PRINT A$(199 to 202) (NEW LINE)
- You should see YOUR

If you have made any errors, check A$ again.

One you have everything in correctly, and A$ in memory, delete line 110. Be sure not to press (CLEAR) or (RUN) from now on.

Program 3:

```
110  FOR I = 1 TO 89
120  LET J = -1
130  LET J = J + 1
140  LET K = PEEK (16513+I)
150  IF K = 0 THEN GOTO 190
160  PRINT A$ (K+J) ;
170  IF A$ (K+J) <> " ▵ " THEN GOTO 130
                  (space)
180  IF K > 0 THEN GOTO 220
190  PRINT "?"
200  INPUT B$
210  CLS
220  NEXT I
```

In order to run this program enter (GOTO 1) (NEW LINE).

IMPROVING THE PROGRAM:

It should be fairly obvious to you by now how to change the conversational patter of the good Doctor: merely redefine new words for the sentences in Program 1. The numbers refer to the position in A$ where the word is stored.

Obviously a great improvement could be made by making the doctor responsive to the player's replies.

This could be achieved in a system with more memory by adding lines such as the following:

```
105  LET C$ = ""
205  IF I = 19 THEN LET C$ = B$
215  IF C$ <> "" THEN PRINT C$;"△";
```

This will add the name of the player in front of the questions, for example.

CAVES AND PITFALLS

(c) by Clifford Ramshaw

"Caves and Pitfalls" is an attempt to bring to the user of the Sinclair ZX 81 a mini-adventure within the confines of a 1K machine.

Naturally this means a loss of many of the nicer things in traditional Adventure games, such as predefined pathways and creatures.

We have to rely entirely on the use of the RND function in this game, and even then it is a very tight squeeze indeed.

The program is so difficult to fit into 1K that it has been found necessary to break the program up into two :

The first program defines all the variables, and after we (RUN) this program we can delete the listing. All the variables will still be remembered in the memory.

The second program is the one that actually controls the game. Because we need the variables we saved from the first program, we cannot (RUN) it ((RUN) destroys all variables in memory), but must use (GOTO 1) instead.

The other major space saving used in this program is to try to eliminate numbers from the listing of the program. Any number in a program listing, whether something like "FOR X = 1 TO 3" or something like "LET S = 16384", will use up 6 bytes of memory.

This is obviously very wasteful for single and double digit numbers and we have used variables defined in the first program to get over this.

VARIABLES USED IN THE PROGRAM:

We define all the fixed variables in the first program. These are:

Monsters we may meet: These are stored in "A$" which is dimensioned as 4 strings of up to 6 characters each.

Treasure we can find: These are stored in "B$" which is dimensioned as 2 strings of 6 characters each.

Factors which define the score: These are "T" which is the value of treasure found, and "K" which is the number of monsters killed. The score is obtained by multiplying these two.

Numbers used in the second program: 1,2,3,5,10.

CAVES AND PITFALLS

Program 1

```
100  DIM A$(4,6)
110  LET A$(1) = "DRAGON"
120  LET A$(2) = "ZOMBIE"
130  LET A$(3) = "WRAITH"
140  LET A$(4) = "HYDRA"
150  DIM B$(2,6)
160  LET B$(1) = "GOLD"
170  LET B$(2) = "SILVER"
180  LET T = 0
190  LET K = 0
200  LET X = 1
```

```
210  LET R = 2
220  LET Y = 3
230  LET Z = 5
240  LET W = 10
```

You must (RUN) this program before you can delete this listing and continue with entering program 2.

After you have (RUN) this program, you may be interested to see how much space it is possible to save by this method of predefining variables. Enter the following line without a line number:

```
PRINT PEEK 16404 + 256 * PEEK 16405
```

This will give you the position of the end of the variable file, and should be about 16900.

Now delete all this listing by entering the lines numbers followed by (NEW LINE). You will end up with a blank screen. To check that all the variables are still remembered you can enter

```
PRINT A$(1)
```

When you press (NEW LINE) you will see DRAGON on the screen! By entering the line as above to check on memory usage, you will see that we have saved about 300 bytes of program listing, without losing any of the variables!

CAVES AND PITFALLS

Program 2

Important note:

You cannot enter Program 2 without having entered program 1, (RUN) program 1, and deleted its

listing as above.
Also do not press (CLEAR) or (RUN) at any stage while entering Program 2 as this will destroy the variables saved.

```
100  GOSUB 800
110  PRINT "LEFT,RIGHT?"
120  INPUT A
130  CLS
140  GOTO W * W * INT (R * R * RND + X)
200  PRINT "A DOOR" ,, "LEAVE OR IN?"
210  INPUT A
220  IF A = X THEN GO TO W * W
300  PRINT "YOU SEE A△"; A$( INT (R * R * RND)
       + X) , "IT ADVANCES"
310  GOTO 500
400  PRINT "WHOOPS...A PIT"
410  LET A = INT (W * RND + X)
420  IF A = X THEN GO TO W * W
430  PRINT "AT THE BOTTOM△";
440  IF A < Y THEN GOTO 300
450  PRINT "ARE△"; A ; "△SPIKES"
460  LET T = T - A
470  GOTO W * W
500  PRINT "FIGHT OR FLEE?"
510  INPUT A
520  CLS
530  IF A <> X THEN GOTO W * W
540  LET A = W * RND
550  IF A >= Y THEN GOTO 600
560  PRINT "RIP"
570  GOTO 800
600  IF A > Z THEN GO TO 700
610  PRINT "LOST"
620  LET T = INT (T/R)
630  GOTO W * W
700  PRINT "MONSTER IS DEAD"
710  LET K = K + X
720  LET A = R * RND + X
730  PRINT "FOUND△";B$(INT A)
740  LET T = T + INT (A * W * RND + X)
```

```
750  GOTO W * W
800  PRINT "SCORE △";T * K
810  RETURN
```

Note: You may have noticed that the line numbers do not follow an orderly sequence. This is deliberately so, so that the GOTO statement in line 140 can be used.

RUNNING THE PROGRAM:

As mentioned above, we cannot use (RUN) with this program as doing so will destroy all the variables which were so carefully defined.

We must therefore use (GOTO 1) instead.

At each step of the mini-adventure, you will be given a choice of two :

```
TURN LEFT OR TURN RIGHT ?
GO THROUGH THE DOOR OR NOT ?
FIGHT THE MONSTER OR FLEE ?
```

The program is looking for an input of "1" or "2", signifying that you have picked choice 1 or 2.

The game terminates when you have been killed by one of the monsters.
Should you wish to fight another round of "Caves and Pitfalls", you will need to reinitialise the treasure and kill count.

Enter the following lines (without line numbers) to start again:

```
LET T = 0 (NEW LINE)
LET K = 0 (NEW LINE)
GOTO 1    (NEW LINE)
```

Best of luck against the demons of the caverns!

DRAUGHTS

It is possible for the standard 1K Sinclair ZX 81 to play draughts!

Of course, this is only possible by using every trick in the book, including resorting to machine language programming for the part of the program that plays against the human player.

The board is shown on the screen as follows:

```
1     1  B     B     B     B
2     B     B     B     B
3     3  B     B     B     B
4     ▓     ▓     ▓     ▓
5     5  ▓     ▓     ▓     ▓
6     W     W     W     W
7     7  W     W     W     W
8     W     W     W     W

      A  B  C  D  E  F  G  H
```

(The outer numbers 1 - 8 and the designation of columns A - H are not shown on the screen - the only numbering included are the numbers 1,3,5 and 7 as shown within the board).

The rules of the game the ZX 81 plays follow the standard rules except that multiple jumps are not allowed and capture is not compulsory.

Reaching the end line results in the creation of a king (shown on the screen as inverse letter), which can only move one square at a time but is allowed to jump backwards.

STRUCTURE OF THE PROGRAM:

As mentioned above, the board is displayed on the screen - this is the only record the ZX81 has of the state of play! No other array is required to keep track of the game.

This therefore requires the use of PEEKs to find out where the pieces are and POKEs to move them.

In the standard 1K version there is also insufficient room to retain the string variable that initially sets up the board in the program listing. We must therefore resort to putting that string variable in memory and using (GOTO 1) to start the program.

The last space saving "trick" involves replacing all 1- and 2-digit numbers in the listing: each number in a ZX81 listing takes up 6 bytes! This is true even if your number is only a single digit. We therefore make liberal use of constructs such as VAL"2" or CODE"W" which ony require 4 bytes.

The program is also broken down into 3 different programs, the last two of which overlay the previous ones. This is the only way to enter so much information into the Sinclair ZX81 1K.

The structure is as follows:

```
Program 1    PUT MACHINE CODE ROUTINE
               INTO REM STATEMENT
Program 2:   DEFINE THE BOARD FOR PLAY
Program 3:   DRAW THE BOARD
             INPUT PLAYER'S MOVE
             CHECK PLAYER MOVE VALIDITY
             MAKE COMPUTER'S MOVE
               (CALL TO USR ROUTINE)
             GO TO NEXT PLAYER INPUT
```

DRAUGHTS:
=========

PROGRAM 1:

```
 100 REM 111111111111111111111111
111111111222222222222222222222222
222222222333333333333333333333333
333333333444444444444444444444444
444444444555555555555555555555555
55555555566666666666666666
 150 LET S = 16514
 160 FOR I = 0 TO 174
 170 SCROLL
 180 PRINT I;
 190 INPUT A$
 200 IF A$ = "" THEN STOP
 210 LET V = 16 * CODE A$ + CODE A$(2)
   - 476
 220 POKE S+I, V
 230 PRINT TAB 5; A$
 240 NEXT I
```

The REM statement must have 175 chars in it.

This program will input the machine language code into the REM statement. When you (RUN) this program, the screen will show the number, and waits for you to input the code. If you make an error, just enter (NEW LINE) to stop the program, and start again.

The code is on one page at the end of this program. Note that the code to be entered can only contain the letters A - F and the numbers 0 to 9. (It should take you less than 15 minutes to enter this code into the array).

Once you have (RUN) Program 1, the machine language code will be stored in the REM statement in line 100. The listing of program 1 is no longer required. Save the program you have made

so far on to tape and delete lines 150 - 240.

DRAUGHTS

PROGRAM 2

At this stage you should have only line 100 from the program above containing the machine code. Add the following lines:

```
120  LET A$ = "1 B Δ B Δ B Δ B B Δ B Δ B Δ B Δ
 3 B Δ B Δ B Δ B ▦ Δ ▦ Δ ▦ Δ ▦ Δ 5 ▦ Δ ▦ Δ ▦ Δ
▦ W Δ W Δ W Δ W Δ 7 W Δ W Δ W Δ W W Δ W Δ W Δ
 W Δ "
```

The graphics character is obtained by using GRAPHICS and (Shift) (A)

```
150  FOR L = VAL "1" TO VAL "8"
160  PRINT A$ ( TO VAL "8" )
170  LET A$ = A$ ( VAL "9" TO )
180  NEXT L
200  INPUT A$
310  IF USR 16514 > VAL "0" THEN GOTO 200
```

This program will display the board on to the screen and test the machine language routine entered in Program 1.

The screen is saved in the string variable A$, and is printed in 8 lines. It is essential that a minimum configuration screen is set up, so that the structure in memory of the board is as follows:

1 B Δ B Δ B Δ B [&] B Δ B Δ B Δ B Δ [&] 3 ...

(where the symbol [&] is used to represent END-OF-LINE). If you check this out this means that all legal moves are limited to increases and decreases of 8 or 10 bytes in memory.

Users with additional memory connected to the ZX81 should add the following lines:

```
     130  POKE 16389, 76
     140  CLS
```

This will ensure that a minimum configuration screen is set up.

Running Program 2:

After SAVEing the program, press (RUN). You can choose to be in either SLOW or FAST mode. The screen will be displayed as shown at the beginning, and the ZX81 will be waiting for a string input. Press (NEW LINE) to see the computer's first move. You should see the computer move its first piece from G3 to H4.

You can continue to press (NEW LINE) to see what the computer would do next if that was its position. If you so desire you can change the string variable in 120 to set up any starting position.

Preparing for Program 3:

Enter the following line into your listing:

```
        130 STOP
```

and then press (RUN). Delete lines 120 and 130 and SAVE your program so far.

This has the effect of storing the string variable in memory without the need to keep it in the program listing. (Users with more than 1K memory do not need to do this - retain your original lines 120 - 140)

DRAUGHTS

PROGRAM 3

At this stage you should have lines 100, lines 150 - 180, and lines 200 and 310. The string variable A$ is stored in memory, so do not press (RUN) or (CLEAR) as this will destroy the contents of A$.

Add the following lines to your program:

```
210  LET S = PEEK 16396 + VAL "256" * PEEK 16397
220  LET F = S + CODE A$ + VAL "9" * CODE A$ (
   VAL "2" ) - VAL "298"
230  LET T = S + CODE A$ ( VAL "3" ) + VAL "9" *
   CODE A$ ( VAL "4" ) - VAL "298"
240  LET M = (T + F) / VAL "2"
250  IF (PEEK F <> CODE "W" AND PEEK F <> CODE
  "[W]") OR (ABS (F-T) > VAL "10" AND PEEK M <>
  CODE "B" AND PEEK M <> CODE "[B]") OR (PEEK F
  < CODE "X" AND F<T) OR PEEK T <> CODE "▦" THEN
  GOTO 200
```

Letters in squares are inverse characters obtained using GRAPHICS mode.

```
270  POKE T, CODE "W" + CODE "■" * (PEEK F >
  CODE "W" OR (T-S) < VAL "9")
```

The graphic character in this line is obtained in GRAPHICS mode by pressing (Space)

```
280  POKE F, CODE "▦"       This is Graphics A
290  IF ABS (F-T) > VAL "10" THEN POKE M,
  CODE "▦"
300  PAUSE CODE "W"
```

You may find some difficulty in entering the long lines, such as line 250, if you only have 1K of memory. A good hint is to enter (CLS) and (NEW LINE). This does not effect the variables but gives you more room on the screen to enter your line.

SAVE this program before trying to play draughts.

PLAYING DRAUGHTS:

As we mentioned at the beginning, if you only have 1K you cannot use (RUN) as this will clear the variable so carefully saved. Use (GOTO 1) instead. (Users with additional memory have the string variable in the listing so can use (RUN).)

You should already have tested Program 2 by the time you come to this point, so you already know the display routine works and the computer playing routine works.

The additions in Program 3 are the player's moves and checking if these moves are allowed (This is all in line 250: "F" is "from" and "T" is "to". We check to see is the move from contains a White piece, the move to is empty, any captured squares do in fact contain a Black piece, and so on).

The input the computer is waiting for is a 4-character string, such as "A6B5". This means that you mean to move from square A6 to square B5.

As only the most rudimentary numbering has been included in the screen, you may find it useful to keep a properly numbered board by the computer when playing.

The ZX81's response is extremely fast - almost instantaneous as it is written in machine language - so a short delay (line 300) has been introduced to allow you to see the computer's move being made. You can choose to play in either FAST or SLOW mode.

If you should wish to play a second game, you cannot simply use (GOTO 1) again, as the string variable A$ has been deleted from memory. You will need to either reload the program from cassette or re-enter on the edit line the string variable A$ as in line 120 (but without the line number). You can use this to also enter different set positions you wish to examine - eg. giving the computer a head start, etc.

MACHINE LANGUAGE:

As mentioned in the beginning, the part of the program which determines the computer's next move is written in machine language.

We have already seen in the Line Renumbering program and in Machine Code Editor program that using machine language can result in an enormous saving in memory.

This is the reason this part of the program was written in machine language - the validation of the player's move in the above program takes as much room as the entire section dealing with the computer's move: searching for best moves, watching out for traps, making the moves, converting to Kings if required, and so on.

Unfortunately it is beyond the scope of this book to give an explanation of how this particular machine language program works, or how to write improvements for it.

Sll this information can be found in our book "MACHINE LANGUAGE PROGRAMMING MADE SIMPLE". That book also includes a full description of this Draughts program. Price and ordering details are at the back of this book.

0 =	AF	50 =	40	100 =	EB	150 =	42
	21		23		E5		40
	3C		10		ED		E1
	40		DA		52		22
	06		11		E1		44
	0A		3C		38		40
	77		40		02		E1
	23		21		F6		22
	10		43		80		40
	FC		40		77		40
10 =	06	60 =	34	110 =	C9	160 =	C9
	48		35		E5		3A
	2A		01		19		3F
	0C		04		7E		40
	40		00		FE		A7
	E5		20		08		28
	7E		02		20		D8
	FE		0E		12		E1
	A7		00		E5		E1
	28		D5		19		C9
20 =	12	70 =	D5	120 =	7E	170 =	5E
	FE		E1		E6		23
	27		09		7F		56
	20		0E		FE		EB
	1A		04		3C	174 =	C9
	11		ED		28		
	C8		B0		22		
	C0		CD		E1		
	CD		2C		22		
	F1		41		3E		
30 =	40	80 =	36	130 =	40		
	11		08		E1		
	0A		E1		22		
	00		CD		3C		
	CD		2C		40		
	F1		41		C9		
	40		7E		E6		
	18		36		7F		
	0C		08		FE		
	11		13		3C		
40 =	F6	90 =	EB	140 =	20		
	FF		CD		1A		
	CD		2C		E5		
	F1		41		19		
	40		D1		7E		
	11		01		FE		
	F8		3F		08		
	FF		00		20		
	CD		EB		12		
	F1		09		22		

ZX81 ZX81

SINCLAIR

SOFTWARE

ZX81 ZX81

MACHINE LANGUAGE MADE SIMPLE

MACHINE LANGUAGE PROGRAMMING MADE SIMPLE :

This is the book you have been waiting for - the one which will explain in simple and easy terms exactly how to get more power out of the computer. Go beyond BASIC into the world of machine language programming and open computer horizons you never thought possible!

MORE COMPUTING POWER

Now at last you can use the full potential of the heart of the Sinclair ZX81 - the powerful Z80 microprocessor - by creating your own fast machine language programs or subroutines.

Machine Language Made Simple is easy to use and designed for the complete beginner: No other knowledge of programming is required.

* Includes the machine code listing of the Draughts game found in this book, commented and explained, as well as other programs and examples.

FASTER RUNNING PROGRAMS!

Understanding Your ZX81 ROM

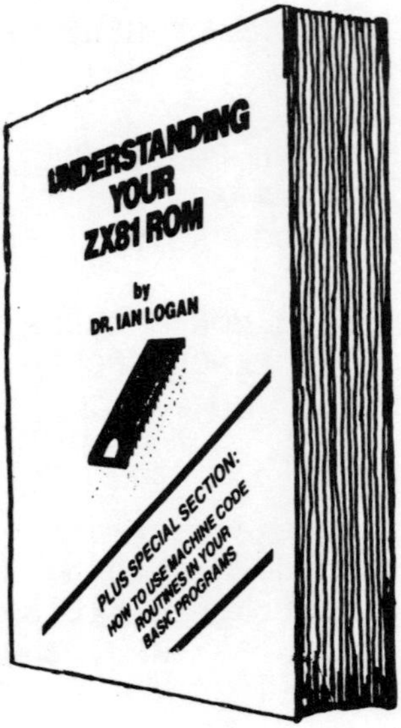

INCLUDES SPECIAL SECTION: How to use machine code routines in your BASIC programs.

Dr. Ian Logan was the first person to dissassemble the ZX80 monitor and now he is the first to explain exactly how the Sinclair ZX81 ROM does what it does.

Full details on the structure of the ROM are given, including the way the Sinclair ZX81 handles the display, the cassette, and the keyboard!

ROM addresses for all major ROM routines are given. This makes it easy to write your own specific programs using the ROM's routines.

This is an essential book for those who really want to understand the full working of the Sinclair ZX81.

ORDERING DETAILS:

ORDERS FOR PUBLICATIONS OF MELBOURNE HOUSE SHOULD BE SENT TO :

MELBOURNE HOUSE PUBLISHERS
131 TRAFALGAR ROAD
GREENWICH LONDON SE10

ENCLOSING A CHEQUE OR MONEY ORDER. A POST AND PACKING CHARGE OF 80 PENCE SHOULD BE ADDED TO THE COSTS OF THE BOOKS.

Any correspondance regarding any of these titles should be addressed to Melbourne House Publishers, Glebe Cottage, Station Road, Cheddington, Leighton Buzzard, Beds. LU7 7NA.

Titles available:

THE COMPLETE ZX81 BASIC COURSE	£17.50
BASIC Course Programs on Cassette	£ 2.50
NOT ONLY 30 PROGRAMS FOR ZX81 1K	£ 6.95
MACHINE LANGUAGE MADE SIMPLE (ZX81)	£ 8.95
UNDERSTANDING YOUR ZX81 ROM	£ 8.95